1/13

as a fit and necessa...

effecting this object,

chief of the Army and

...tes, do ... and des-

...t day of January in the

...housand eight hundred

...held as slaves with

...therein the Constitution:

...ted States, shall not

...nized, submitted

then, thenceforward and

be, prosecuted. As a
ry military measure
, as Commander-in-
Navy of the United
clare that on the fi
year of our Lord one
and sixty-three, all p
in any State or States,
al authority of the li
then be practically re
and maintained, sha
forever, be free,

EMANCIPATION PROCLAMATION

EMANCIPATION PROCLAMATION

LINCOLN *and the* DAWN *of* LIBERTY

TONYA BOLDEN

ABRAMS BOOKS FOR YOUNG READERS · NEW YORK

for **HOWARD REEVES,**
who truly cares about those
agonizing prayers of centuries

This book grew out of my article "The Trump of Jubilee," published in ASALH's
2007 edition of *The Woodson Review.*

Library of Congress Cataloging-in-Publication Data

Bolden, Tonya.
Emancipation Proclamation : Lincoln and the dawn of liberty / Tonya Bolden.
p. cm.
Includes bibliographical references and index.
ISBN 978-1-4197-0390-4 (alk. paper)
1. United States. President (1861–1865 : Lincoln). Emancipation Proclamation—Juvenile literature.
2. Lincoln, Abraham, 1809–1865—Juvenile literature. 3. Slaves—Emancipation—United States—
Juvenile literature. 4. United States—Politics and government—1861–1865—Juvenile literature. I. Title.
E453.B68 2012
973'.7.14—dc23
2012000845

Text copyright © 2013 Tonya Bolden
For illustration credits, see page 112.
Book design by Maria T. Middleton

Printed and bound in China
10 9 8 7 6 5 4 3 2 1

Abrams Books for Young Readers are available at special discounts when purchased in quantity for
premiums and promotions as well as fundraising or educational use. Special editions can also be
created to specification. For details, contact specialsales@abramsbooks.com or the address below.

ABRAMS
THE ART OF BOOKS SINCE 1949
115 West 18th Street
New York, NY 10011
www.abramsbooks.com

PREVIOUS PAGE Hilton Head, South Carolina, May 1862. Photograph by Henry P. Moore. The black people
were the property of CSA general Thomas F. Drayton. The white man is most likely a Union soldier.

CONTENTS

A bird's-eye view of Old Point Comfort in Hampton Virginia (1861). The peninsula is dominated by Fort Monroe, known during the Civil War as Freedom's Fort. Lithograph by E. Sachse & Co.

ABRAHAM LINCOLN WAS *perhaps the greatest figure of the nineteenth century. . . . And I love him not because he was perfect but because he was not and yet triumphed. . . .*

[P]ersonally I revere him the more because up out of his contradictions and inconsistencies he fought his way to the pinnacles of earth and his fight was within as well as without.

—W. E. B. Du Bois, *The Crisis* (September 1922)

A HIGHLY SECRETIVE *man, easy to underestimate, whose inner musings were for the most part unknowable, Lincoln remains endlessly fascinating to school children, scholars and all those who view his life in epic terms.*

—Larry Jordan, *Midwest Today* (February 1993)

THE PROBLEM IS *that we tend too often to read Lincoln's growth backward, as an unproblematic trajectory toward a predetermined end. This enables scholars to ignore or downplay aspects of Lincoln's beliefs with which they are uncomfortable.*

—Eric Foner, *The Fiery Trial* (2010)

Tremont Temple, a Baptist church in Boston (ca. 1857). Lithograph by J. H. Bufford.

PART I

"THE AGONIZING PRAYERS OF CENTURIES"

"WE WERE WAITING AND LISTENING AS FOR A BOLT FROM the sky . . . we were watching, as it were, by the dim light of the stars, for the dawn of a new day; we were longing for the answer to the agonizing prayers of centuries."

So remembered Frederick Douglass, speaking of a "we" that included the electric lecturer Anna E. Dickinson, the riveting Reverend J. Sella Martin, and some three thousand other anxious souls packed into Tremont Temple, a Boston church.

This "we" was waiting for word that Abraham Lincoln had John Hancocked a proclamation of liberation.

It was Thursday, January 1, 1863.

Blocks south of Tremont Temple, in snowy Boston's Music Hall, another crowd of abolitionists was waiting. Ralph Waldo Emerson was there. So were William Lloyd Garrison and Harriet Beecher Stowe. Absent from both great gatherings was the relentless Wendell Phillips, a lawyer by trade. He was in nearby Medford, waiting at the home of friends George and Mary Stearns.

———————

ON NEW YEAR'S DAY, 1863, THE WAITING WE WASN'T LIMITED to the Boston area.

Washington, D.C., had Henry McNeal Turner, the pastor of Israel Bethel, a church at the foot of Capitol Hill.

Waiting.

On a farm near Columbus, Ohio, there was the writer Frances E. W. Harper, ever poised to pen another poem.

Waiting.

As was Charlotte Forten, a schoolteacher on a South Carolina sea island, not far from Beaufort, where Harriet Tubman was based.

Waiting.

Just like Sandy Cornish in Key West, Florida, a man who had bought his liberty in the 1840s but who later lost his freedom papers in a fire. Worse, one night Cornish was jumped by fiends intent on selling him back into slavery. By dint of will and brute strength, Cornish broke loose. Then, the next day in the public square, he attacked *himself.*

Cornish slashed his Achilles tendons, drove a knife into a hip, and in other ways butchered his body. All to make himself useless for slavery. As he told the cowed crowd, he was willing to do worse—anything but be "a slave agin, for I was free."

Now, some twenty years later, like others who stood against slavery, the scarred—but free—Sandy Cornish, about seventy, was waiting for that "dawn of a new day."

FOR THE TRUE BELIEVERS in freedom—the enslaved, the freed, and those who had always lived in liberty—it had been a very long wait indeed.

Since 1641, when Massachusetts became England's first North American colony to legalize slavery.

Since 1770, when Crispus Attucks took two musket balls to the chest during the Boston Massacre.

Since black patriots fought so fiercely at the Battle of Lexington and Concord, then at Bunker Hill.

When the Declaration of Independence deemed it "self-evident" that "all men are created equal" and entitled to "life, liberty, and the pursuit of happiness," we waited for the birth of a slavery-free new nation. But that was not to be.

Petition for freedom to Massachusetts governor Thomas Gage, His Majesty's Council, and the House of Representatives, May 25, 1774 (page one). In this document, a great number of blacks stated that they, like all people, had a natural right to freedom. They beseeched the authorities to set them and their children at liberty.

THE U.S. CONSTITUTION AND SLAVERY

The Constitution, completed in September 1787, does not include the words *slave* or *slavery*. The framers, a number of whom were slaveholders, instead used euphemisms. (Example: "person held to service or labor" for someone enslaved.) Parts of the Constitution that address slavery include the following three excerpts. An explanation follows each.

ARTICLE I, SECTION 2

Representatives and direct Taxes shall be apportioned among the several States which may be included within this Union, according to their respective Numbers, which shall be determined by adding to the whole Number of free Persons, including those bound to Service for a Term of Years, and excluding Indians not taxed, three fifths of all other Persons.

For direct taxation and representation in Congress, each enslaved person is to be counted as three-fifths of a person. This allowed states with large populations of enslaved people to have more representation in Congress than if enslaved people weren't counted (as antislavery people wished) but less representation than if the enslaved were counted as whole persons (as slaveholders wanted).

ARTICLE I, SECTION 9

The Migration or Importation of such Persons as any of the States now existing shall think proper to admit, shall not be prohibited by the Congress prior to the Year one thousand eight hundred and eight, but a Tax or duty may be imposed on such Importation, not exceeding ten dollars for each Person.

Congress cannot abolish the slave trade until 1808, and a tax can be levied on the importation of human beings.

ARTICLE IV, SECTION 2

No Person held to Service or Labour in one State, under the Laws thereof, escaping into another, shall, in Consequence of any Law or Regulation therein, be discharged from such Service or Labour, but shall be delivered up on Claim of the Party to whom such Service or Labour may be due.

Escape from slavery to a state prohibiting it does not translate into legal liberty. This "fugitive slave" clause also says that those who flee bondage are to be "delivered up" to their owners.

OVER THE YEARS, WE REJOICED WHEN A NORTHERN STATE abolished the abomination. We agonized when a slave state entered the Union. As the nation grew westward, we fought slavery's spread.

The Missouri Compromise of 1820 was something of a mercy: Maine entered the Union as a free state to offset Missouri's entry as a slave state. Added to that, slavery was banned from the rest of Louisiana Purchase lands (outside of Missouri) located north of the parallel 36°30'.

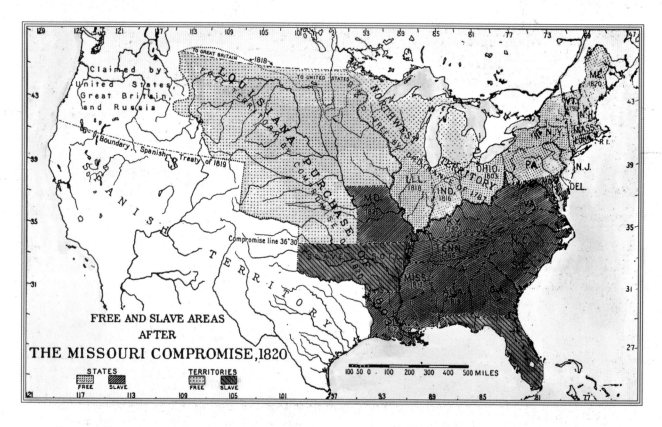

Free and Slave Areas After the Missouri Compromise, 1820. The Missouri Compromise was intended to keep the peace between the North and the South. Along with allowing Maine into the Union as a free state and Missouri as a slave state, the compromise banned slavery in unorganized Louisana Purchase land (originally 800,000-plus square miles). The U.S. bought this land from France in 1803 for fifteen million dollars. Part of the purchase became the state of Louisiana in 1812 and Arkansas Territory in 1819.

The Northwest Territory: Acquired from England in 1783, in the treaty that ended the American Revolution. Congress banned slavery in the Northwest Territory, which originally consisted of present-day Illinois, Indiana, Michigan, Ohio, Wisconsin, and part of Minnesota.

Florida Territory: Acquired from Spain in the Adams-Onís treaty signed in 1819.

As we waited for all of America to repent—to repudiate slavery—we wept, we raged, we prayed. Over beatings and brandings and bullwhippings. Over the rapes. Over families fractured on auction blocks. And then there was all that stolen labor.

A Slave-Coffle Passing the Capitol, from *A Popular History of the United States* (vol. 4, 1881). Slave labor was used to build the White House and the Capitol.

I HAVE OFTEN *been awakened at the dawn of day by the most heart-rending shrieks of [my Aunt Hester], whom [our master, Aaron Anthony] used to tie up to a joist, and whip upon her naked back till she was literally covered with blood. No words, no tears, no prayers, from his gory victim, seemed to move his iron heart. . . . I remember the first time I ever witnessed this horrible exhibition. I was quite a child. . . . It was the blood-stained gate, the entrance to the hell of slavery, through which I was about to pass.*

—Frederick Douglass, in his first autobiography, *Narrative of the Life of Frederick Douglass, An American Slave* (1845), which featured a preface by William Lloyd Garrison and a letter of support from Wendell Phillips

I NEVER RISE *to address a colored audience without feeling ashamed of my own color; ashamed of being identified with a race of men who have done you so much injustice, and who yet retain so large a portion of your brethren in servile chains.*

—William Lloyd Garrison in June 1831, to black conventions in Boston, Philadelphia, and other northern cities

So often we sought solace in freedom songs, like "The Day of Jubilee":

Soon shall the trump of freedom
Resound from shore to shore;
Soon, taught by heavenly wisdom,
Man shall oppress no more:
But every yoke be broken,
Each captive soul set free—
And every heart shall welcome
The day of Jubilee.

LEFT Frederick Douglass (ca.1847–52), by Samuel J. Miller. Maryland-born Douglass liberated himself in 1838, when he was twenty. During the Civil War, Douglass and his family lived in Rochester, New York.

RIGHT William Lloyd Garrison (ca. 1850), by Southworth & Hawes. Massachusetts-born Garrison was the founding editor of *The Liberator* (1831) and president of the American Anti-Slavery Society from 1843 to 1865. Garrison once supported gradual emancipation and the colonization of blacks outside America. After a change of heart, he became a leading voice for immediate, unconditional abolition and against colonization.

All the while, we waited for breakthroughs from piles of appeals on behalf of black humanity: all the books and broadsides, pamphlets and petitions, articles and ardent speeches; all the people, like Elijah Lovejoy, persecuted—flogged, bludgeoned, hanged, tarred and feathered, shot—for entreating the nation to set the captives free.

ABOVE *The Mob Attacking the Warehouse of Godfrey Gilman & Co., Alton, Ill., on the Night of the 7th Nov. 1837*, from *Alton Trials* (1838). On the night of November 7, 1837, a proslavery mob attacked Gilman's warehouse, on the banks of the Mississippi River, because it held the new printing press of white abolitionist Elijah Lovejoy. The printing press was destroyed and dumped into the river (as had been done to three of Lovejoy's previous presses). Elijah Lovejoy was shot dead while trying to defend his property.

OPPOSITE Western Anti-Slavery Society leaflet (ca. 1850).

Union with Freemen--No Union with Slaveholders.

ANTI-SLAVERY MEETINGS!

Anti-Slavery Meetings will be held in this place, to commence on   at
in the

To be Addressed by

Agents of the Western ANTI-SLAVERY SOCIETY.

Three millions of your fellow beings are in chains--the Church and Government sustains the horrible system of oppression.

Turn Out!

AND LEARN YOUR DUTY TO YOURSELVES, THE SLAVE AND GOD.

EMANCIPATION or DISSOLUTION, and a FREE NORTHERN REPUBLIC!

HOMESTEAD PRINT, SALEM, OHIO.

THE LIBERATOR.

VOL. I.]   WILLIAM LLOYD GARRISON AND ISAAC KNAPP, PUBLISHERS.   [NO. 17.

BOSTON, MASSACHUSETTS.   OUR COUNTRY IS THE WORLD—OUR COUNTRYMEN ARE MANKIND.   [SATURDAY, April 23, 1831.

OUTRAGE.

Fellow Citizens,

AN ABOLITIONIST,

of the most revolting character is among you, exciting the feelings of the North against the South. A seditious Lecture is to be delivered

THIS EVENING,

at 7 o'clock, at the Presbyterian Church in Cannon-street. You are requested to attend and unite in putting down and silencing by peaceable means this tool of evil and fanaticism. Let the rights of the States guaranteed by the Constitution be protected.

Feb. 27, 1837.   The Union forever!

OUR FANATICISM.

ALL MEN
ARE CREATED EQUAL:

THOU SHALT

LOVE THY NEIGHBOR AS THYSELF.

ABOVE From the April 23, 1831, issue of Garrison's newspaper.

TOP RIGHT Anti-abolitionist handbill, 1837. A call to disrupt an antislavery meeting–vilifying the speaker as a "tool of evil and fanaticism."

BOTTOM RIGHT Cotton banner (ca. 1840). Garrison displayed it at antislavery events–proud of his "fanaticism."

Mr Garrison.

The following is a copy of a carefully made list of the petitions which have passed through the hands of the committee of the Boston Female A.S.S.

Weston	214	N. Dennis	101	Salisbury	34
S. Weymouth	262	Gloucester	57	Mansfield	72
Bradford	195	Rowe	37	Peru	117
Mentham	302	Princeton	271	Spencer	161
Lowell	1400 S	Worcester	169	Otis	313
Ashfield	140 S	Millbury	375	Northampton	337
West Stockbridge	91	Natick	242	Andover	217
Dover	80	Reading	264	Saxonville	35
Stoughton	110	Shrewsbury	232	Sudbury	114
Kingston	305	Leicester	165	Deerfield	95
Blandford	150	Buckland	104	Brookline	91
Abington	303	Roxbury	481	Cambridgeport and vicinity	415
New Salem	36	Boylston	100	Dunstable	65
Stoneham	69	Westford	235	Greenfield	73
Gill	114	S. Wilbraham	108	Groton	193
Winchester	226	Rowley	40	Bristol Co	3000
Bernardston	83	Orange	90	West Springfield	38
Byfield	52	Lunenburg	175	Royalston	257
Dalton	151	Hinsdale	56	Weymouth	265
South Deerfield	140	Charlestown	104	Braintree	183
Dedham	53	Ashburnham	320	Quincy	126
E. Medway	147	East Brookfield	45	Shirley	72
Hopkinton	220	Brookfield	79	Carlisle	51
Hubbardston	108	N. Bridgewater	294	Newton Centre	47
Hinsdale	54	Paxton	117	East Needham	38
W. Hawley	61	Becket	139	West Newton	115
		W. Bradford	149	West Needham	115
		Haverhill	464		
		Dorchester	325		
		Warren	38		
		Hanover	91		
	3666		5572		6639
	700				5572
	4366				4366
					16547

THE NORTH STAR.

RIGHT IS OF NO SEX—TRUTH IS OF NO COLOR—GOD IS THE FATHER OF US ALL, AND ALL WE ARE BRETHREN

VOL. I. NO. I.   ROCHESTER, N. Y. FRIDAY, DECEMBER 3, 1847.   WHOLE

A Slave-Hunt, from *Cassell's History of the United States* (vol. 3, ca. 1880).

So many days, so many nights, we awaited news of souls with the strength to self-liberate. Did he—did she—did they—meet with God's speed, or did bloodhounds pick up the scent?

Of course we abhorred the Compromise of 1850's Fugitive Slave Law. This "Bloodhound Law" compelled federal marshals to be in the search-and-seizure business, and it gave them the power to commandeer citizens into slave-hunting posses. What's more, anyone who helped someone escape slavery could face imprisonment of up to six months and a fine of as much as one thousand dollars (about seventeen thousand dollars today).

WE DO NOT *breathe well. There is infamy in the air.*

—Ralph Waldo Emerson on the 1850 Fugitive Slave Law, in an 1851 address in Concord, Massachusetts

The United States Senate, A.D. 1850 (1855), by Peter F. Rothermel, engraved by Robert Whitechurch. Kentucky senator Henry Clay is depicted holding forth on the Compromise of 1850, which he engineered to keep the peace between the North and South, just as he had done thirty years earlier with the Missouri Compromise (when he was Speaker of the House). In addition to the Bloodhound Law, the Compromise of 1850 included the abolition of the slave trade (but not slavery itself) in the nation's capital. It also dealt with the contentious issue of slavery in lands acquired through the U.S.–Mexican War (1846–48). California entered the Union as a free state. The rest was organized into Utah and New Mexico territories, where slavery was to be a matter of popular sovereignty—that is, left up to the settlers.

Senator Clay, a slaveholder, was a cofounder of the American Colonization Society (1816). It promoted the emigration of free and freed blacks, primarily to West Africa.

Detail of a map of America in 1854. The Kansas-Nebraska Act lifted the ban on slavery above the 36°30'
parallel, thus nullifying part of the Missouri Compromise. Since the Missouri Compromise, more of the Louisiana
Purchase lands had become different territories.

We seethed all the more as the outrages went on. In 1854 came the Kansas-
Nebraska Act, so galling, so appalling. It trampled underfoot the Missouri Compromise by making slavery *possible* in these two new territories if that's what
settlers wanted. And it caused a civil war in one territory between proslavery
and antislavery activists, resulting in "Bleeding Kansas."

There was also "Bleeding Sumner": Massachusetts Senator Charles Sumner, nearly beaten to death—on the Senate floor!—by Representative Preston Brooks of South Carolina. At the heart of Brooks's hatred was Sumner's diehard antislavery stance.

SOUTHERN CHIVALRY _ ARGUMENT versus CLUB'S.

Southern Chivalry–Argument Versus Club's [sic] (1856), by John L. Magee. On May 22, 1856, Representative Brooks attacked Senator Sumner with his gutta-percha cane in the Senate chamber. Sumner had recently given his speech "Crime Against Kansas" denouncing efforts to make Kansas slave soil. He also insulted Brooks's state and his relative, South Carolina Senator Andrew Butler. After the incident, Brooks received gifts of several new canes. The one from a Virginia chamber of commerce and the one from a group of citizens in Charleston, South Carolina, were inscribed: "Hit Him Again." Sumner didn't return to the Senate for three years because of his injuries.

HOW LONG WILL *Northern men watch this struggle between Freedom and Slavery? . . . How long will they see their rights trampled on, their liberty sacrificed, their highest and most lofty sentiments crushed beneath the iron heel of oppression! How long will they bear all this without one effort of resistance?*

—Thirteen-year-old Anna E. Dickinson, in a January 1856 letter to *The Liberator.* She was distraught over news that a schoolteacher in Lexington, Kentucky, had been tarred and feathered for protesting slavery.

Many of us put great faith in the fledgling Republican Party, born of protest over the Kansas-Nebraska Act and dedicated to banning slavery in the territories. We especially cheered the "radicals": Republicans intent on seeing slavery abolished *everywhere* in America.

The Republican Party's chief competition was the Democratic Party, a party dominated by proslavery Southerners, a party with more than a few Northern members on the side of wealthy planters who craved virgin land out west on which to build more slave-worked plantations.

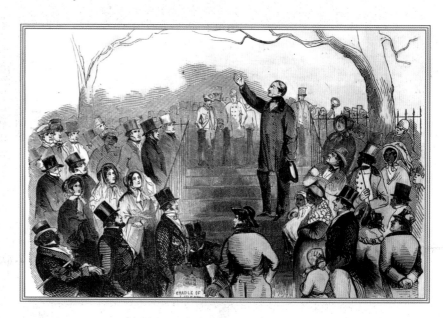

Anti-Slavery Meeting on the Common, by Worcester & Pierce, from the May 3, 1851, issue of *Gleason's Pictorial Drawing-Room Companion.* It depicts Wendell Phillips speaking at an April 11, 1851, rally in Boston over the arrest, under the Fugitive Slave Law, of bricklayer Thomas Simms ("Sims" in some sources). He was soon returned to slavery in Savannah, Georgia.

G. H. Hayes's engraving of "the Sack of Lawrence," a free-soil stronghold in Kansas Territory. The town was destroyed by proslavery activists on May 21, 1856. A few days later, abolitionist John Brown captained the massacre of several proslavery men living near Lawrence, along Pottawatomie Creek.

In 1856, the man the Republican Party fielded for the presidency was the former explorer of the American West known as "the Pathfinder": Colonel John Charles Frémont.

His slogan thrilled: "Free Soil, Free Labor, Free Speech, Free Men, and Frémont!" But in the end, the next president was a Democrat, James Buchanan of Pennsylvania.

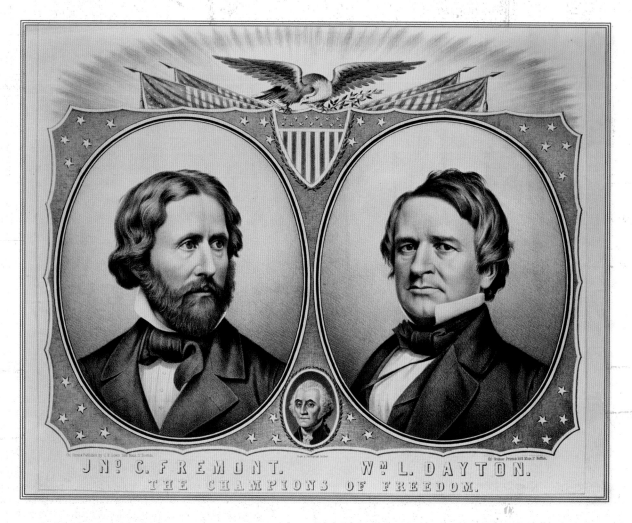

Jno C. Fremont [and] Wm. L. Dayton. The Champions of Freedom! (ca. 1856). Frémont's running mate, featured in this Republican Party presidential campaign banner, was William Lewis Dayton of New Jersey, a former U.S. senator.

In March 1857, two days after Buchanan's inauguration, came another blow: the U.S. Supreme Court's Dred Scott decision, denying liberty to Dred and Harriet Scott, enslaved in St. Louis, Missouri. The couple had sued for freedom on the grounds that, at times, their owner had them in captivity on free soil (for one, at Fort Snelling in Wisconsin Territory, where the two met and married).

The Supreme Court's 7–2 decision did more than say no to the Scotts' freedom plea. It rejected the notion that they had a right to sue in the first place. Whatever blacks' hopes and dreams were, they didn't matter. Blacks really had no rights, said Chief Justice Roger Brooke Taney. Whether enslaved or free, blacks never were and could never be U.S. citizens: They were not included in the Constitution's "We the people."

Going farther afield, Chief Justice Taney also declared that the federal government had no right to regulate slavery in the territories.

WE ARE HERE *to enter our indignant protest against the Dred Scott decision—against the infamous Fugitive Slave Law—against all unjust and oppressive enactments . . . against the alarming aggression of the Slave Power upon the rights of the people of the North—and especially against the existence of the slave system at the South. . . . We are here to reiterate the self-evident truths of the Declaration of Independence. . . . We are here to declare that the men who, like Crispus Attucks, were ready to lay down their lives to secure American Independence, and the blessings of liberty . . . are not the men to be denied the claims of human nature, or the rights of citizenship. . . .*

Give us Disunion with liberty and a good conscience, rather than Union with slavery and moral degradation.

—William Lloyd Garrison at Boston's Faneuil Hall, March 5, 1858, during a commemoration of the Boston Massacre

---

The abolitionist John Brown was all the more on fire after the Dred Scott decision, envisioning a mighty uprising against slavery. Financed by a group known as the Secret Six, he sought to set off the revolt in October 1859. His trigger: an audacious attack on the federal arsenal at Harpers Ferry, Virginia.

After the raid failed, the name "John Brown" became both a rallying cry and a lightning rod. More so after he was captured, tried, and found guilty of conspiracy, murder, and treason, then executed by the Commonwealth of Virginia on December 2, 1859, a day we sorely mourned.

I KNOW THAT *there is some quibbling, some querulousness, some fear, in reference to an out-and-out endorsement of [John Brown's] course . . . but I am prepared, my friends . . . to approve of the means . . . because I remember that our Fourth-of-July orators sanction the same thing; because I remember that Concord, and Bunker Hill . . . and the celebration of those events, all go to approve the means that John Brown has used; the only difference being, that in our battles, in America, means have been used for* white *men and that John Brown has used his means for* black *men. . . .*

I am ready to say, if he has violated the law . . . if he has been the traitor that the South brands him as having been, and the madman that the North says he has been, John Brown is not to be blamed. I say that the system which violates the sacredness of conjugal love, the system that robs the cradle of its innocent treasure . . . the system that takes away every God-given right . . . I say that that system is responsible for every single crime committed within the borders where [slavery] exists. It is the system, my friends.

—J. Sella Martin, before a crowd of four thousand blacks and whites at Boston's Tremont Temple, on the day of John Brown's execution

---

A photograph of John Brown by J. B. Heywood and painted by N. B. Onthank. The photograph was taken in May 1859, five months before Brown's Harpers Ferry raid. The proslavery mob's murder of Elijah Lovejoy in 1837 played a role in Brown's commitment—body, soul, and mind—to abolition and equal rights for blacks.

About a year after John Brown's body dangled from a rope, a Republican won the White House: Abraham Lincoln of Illinois. He was a man on record as calling slavery a "monstrous injustice."

On election night 1860, we who were pledged to universal liberty wondered if the wait would soon be over.

GREAT SALE

OF

LAND, NEGROES,

CORN, &

OTHER PROPERTY!

Pursuant to a decree of the Chancery Court

of Sumter County, I, as Administrator of Hamilton Houston, deceased, will sell at the late residence of John Houston, deceased, one mile west of Warsaw, on Wednesday, the 2d day of January next, the following valuable property:

The Tract of Land occupied by John Houston at the time of his death, containing about 1664 ACRES, and composed of the following subdivisions:

S. E. quarter of S. 6, T. 22, R. 2, West,	160 acres.	R. 2, West,	160 acres.	Fractional S. 32, T. 23, R. 2, West,	620 acres.
E. half of S. W. quarter of S. 6, T. 22, R. 2, West,	80 "	E. half of S. W. quarter of S. 31, T. 23, R. 2, West, S. E. quarter of N. E. qr. of	80 "	E. half of S. W. quarter of S. 29, T. 23, R. 2, West,	80 "
N. half of S. 6, T. 22, R. 2, West,	320 "	S. 31, T. 23, R. 2, West, W. half of N. E. quarter of S.	40 "	Fraction near Jamestown, in S. 29, T. 23, R. 2, West,	44 "
S. E. quarter of S. 31, T. 23,		31, T. 23, R. 2, West,	80 "		

ALSO,

91 LIKELY NEGROES,

SOME OF WHICH ARE BLACKSMITHS AND OTHERS CARPENTERS!

About 6000 bushels of Corn; about 60,000 or 70,000 lbs. of Fodder; 100 Pork Hogs; 200 Sows, Pigs, and Shoats; 11 Cows and Calves; 26 Head of Cattle; 13 Oxen; 24 Mules; 1 Pony; 1 Horse; 1 Bed and Furniture; 1 Book Case; 1 Wash Stand and Contents; 1 Wardrobe and Contents; 6 Chairs; 1 Rocking Chair; 1 Trunk; 1 Valise; 1 Looking Glass; 1 Carpet; 1 Small Table; 1 pair Andirons; 1 small lot of Crockery; 1 lot of Cooking Utensils; 2 Kettles; 1 Buggy and Harness; 8 Bee Hives; 3 sets of Carpenter's Tools; 1 Whip-Saw; 2 Cross Cut Saws; 4 Buster Ploughs; 70 Sweeps and Ploughs; 1 Horse Cart; 3 Ox Wagons; 1 Two-Horse Wagon; 20 Axes; 1 lot of Weeding Hoes; 1 lot of Plough Gear; 1 Doubled barrelled Gun; 1 Corn Mill; 1 Cotton Gin and Band; 1 lot of Lumber; 1 set of Blacksmith's Tools; 1 lot of iron; 20 new Ploughs; 4 new Sweeps—and a large lot of Cotton Seed.

The Sale will commence at 12 o'clock, and be continued until 5, and be continued within those hours from day to day, until completed.

The undersigned, or the overseer on the place, will show the Land to any one who wishes to examine it, at any time before the sale.

TERMS OF SALE:

The Land will be sold on a credit of one and two years, with interest from the day of sale; and the purchaser, or purchasers, will be required to give notes with at least two good securities, for the purchase money. A certificate of purchase will be given to the purchaser, or purchasers, providing for a title to be made when the purchase-money shall be paid.

All the other property will be sold on a credit of twelve months, with interest from the day of sale,—purchasers giving notes with at least two good securities.

WILLIS V. HARE,
Administrator of Hamilton Houston.

November 24th, 1860.

PART II

"A FIT AND NECESSARY MILITARY MEASURE"

THE ENIGMATIC, MOODY, PRONE-TO-BROODING ABRAHAM Lincoln, like most whites of his day, didn't think blacks (or any people of color) rated full equality, but he did believe that all people had a right to the fruits of their own labor. He truly loathed slavery. He saw it as plain *wrong*—and a blot on the nation, an anathema to its ideals.

Problem was, as lawyer Lincoln interpreted the Constitution, the U.S. government could not regulate an institution within a state, be that institution marriage or slavery. Too, Lincoln couldn't turn a blind eye to the Fifth Amendment's provision barring the government from seizing people's property (whether land, home, or human beings) without compensation—that is, payment.

"I have no purpose directly or indirectly to interfere with the institution of slavery in the states where it exists. I believe I have no lawful right to do so, and I have no inclination to do so." Lincoln had uttered these words in 1858 during a senatoral election debate with the father of the Kansas-Nebraska Act, Senator Stephen Douglas of Illinois (whom Lincoln failed to unseat).

Two years later, while seeking to be the Republican Party's presidential candidate, Lincoln held fast to his equally long-held belief that, though the U.S. government could not regulate slavery in the states, it *could* regulate it in the territories. He would point out, for example, that back in 1787 Congress banned slavery in the Northwest Territory.

Lincoln made this point in his February 1860 speech at New York City's Cooper Institute. There he held the packed Great Hall for two hours and closed with this charge: "Let us have faith that right makes might, and in that faith, let us, to the end, dare to do our duty as we understand it."

This speech brought Lincoln to national prominence, and he clinched the Republican Party's presidential nomination a few months later.

Legions of proslavery Southerners—especially wealthy planters—believed that it was their duty to leave the Union if Lincoln became president. They were dead sure that he wouldn't just continue to rail against slavery in the territories, he would also seek to abolish it in the states where it already existed, despite what he said.

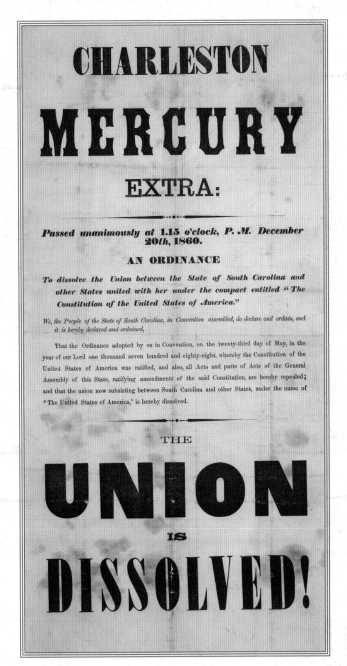

LEFT "The Union Is Dissolved!" *Charleston Mercury*, December 20, 1860. The first public notice that the South Carolina legislature had voted unanimously to leave the Union.

After Lincoln won the White House, South Carolina proved that disunion had been no idle threat. In December 1860—three months before Lincoln was even inaugurated—South Carolina issued its declaration of independence.

By early February 1861 more states had seceded: Mississippi, Florida, Alabama, Georgia, Louisiana, then Texas.

CSA president Jefferson Davis (ca.1858–60), by Mathew Brady. Like Lincoln, Davis was born in the slave state of Kentucky. His pre–Civil War career in the U.S. government included service as secretary of war and as a U.S. senator from Mississippi, a post he quit after that state left the Union in January 1861.

The breakaway states formed the Confederate States of America (CSA), creating a government that paralleled that of the United States, having a legislative, a judicial, and an executive branch. Its chief executive was Jefferson Davis, a Mississippi planter and slaveholder.

The CSA's constitution pulled no punches on slavery. It stated that in any new territory that the Confederacy acquired "the institution of negro slavery, as it now exists in the Confederate States, shall be recognized and protected." And from the start, the CSA was keen on seizing U.S. property within its borders, especially arsenals and forts.

A divided America couldn't wait to hear what Lincoln had to say on March 4, 1861, Inauguration Day. In his speech, Lincoln reached for reconciliation, striving to stave off a civil war and to keep the remaining slave states from joining the CSA.

He reiterated that he had no plans or desire to interfere with slavery in the states. He promised that the U.S. government would continue to uphold the 1850 Fugitive Slave Law. He also mentioned a measure that the outgoing president, James Buchanan, had promoted and that Congress had passed two days earlier: a thirteenth amendment to the Constitution that would ban Congress from ever abolishing slavery in the states where it already existed.

"I have no objection to its being made express, and irrevocable," said Lincoln of this amendment.

I KNOW WHAT *anarchy is. I know what civil war is. I can imagine the scenes of blood through which a rebellious slave population must march to their rights. They are dreadful. And yet, I do not know, that, to an enlightened mind, a scene of civil war is any more sickening than the thought of a hundred and fifty years of slavery.*

—Wendell Phillips at Boston's Music Hall in mid-February 1861

LEFT *Inauguration of President Lincoln, in Front of the Capitol, at Washington, D.C.*, from the October 1, 1881, issue of *Pictorial War Record*. The Capitol's new dome will not be completed until 1863, when its Statue of Freedom is installed on top. (And not until 1937 will Inauguration Day be changed from March 4 to January 20.)

ABOVE Boston-born abolitionist Wendell Phillips (ca. 1858).

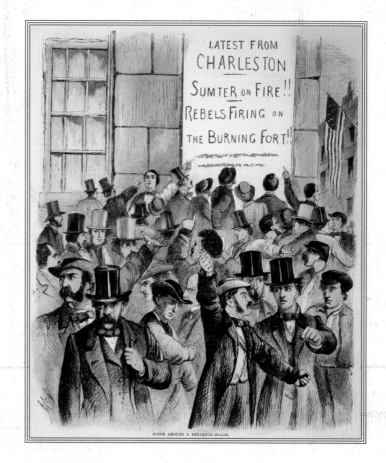

RIGHT *Scene Around a Bulletin-Board*, from *Harper's Pictorial History of the Great Rebellion* (1866). On April 13, 1861, the Union's Major Robert Anderson surrendered Fort Sumter.

OPPOSITE *Interior of Fort Sumter. During the Bombardment, April, 12th, 1861*, by Currier & Ives (1861). The CSA attacked Fort Sumter when the Union moved to resupply it with food and other provisions.

At the end of his inaugural address, Lincoln pressed hard for peace and reunion. "In *your* hands, my dissatisfied fellow-countrymen, and not in *mine*, is the momentous issue of civil war. The government will not assail *you*. You can have no conflict, without being yourselves the aggressors."

He closed on a note of hope: for "the better angels of our nature" to prevail.

About a month later, Confederate forces fired on Union-held Fort Sumter in South Carolina's Charleston Harbor. Soon, the Civil War was on.

By late spring 1861, four more slave states—Virginia, Arkansas, North Carolina, Tennessee—had joined the CSA. Adding to the turmoil, Virginia's western counties, where allegiance to the Union was strong and reliance on slavery was not, had seceded from the Old Dominion (the genesis of a future state: West Virginia).

AS SABERS SLASHED, AS SHOT AND SHELL BLASTED LAND
and obliterated lives, Lincoln steadily proclaimed that the *sole* aim of the war
was to end the rebellion—preserve the Union as it was.

Abolitionists called for a broader war. "Death to Slavery!" was their hearts'
cry—as it was for countless souls in captivity, scores of whom made haste to
Union camps and forts the minute America began flying apart. Fortunate were
the ones given asylum. Most were rebuffed, and some were even returned to
their owners. Similarly, when free black men rushed to fight in the Union Army,
their services were refused.

The Lexington of 1861, Currier & Ives (ca. 1861).
On April 19, 1861, in Baltimore, Maryland, pro-
Confederate people attacked the Union's Sixth
Massachusetts Regiment en route to Washington,
D.C. The incident, in which soldiers and civilians were
wounded and killed, is known as the Baltimore Riot,
the Pratt Street Riot, or the Baltimore Massacre.
Local and state authorities ordered certain railroad
bridges destroyed to prevent more federal troops
from traveling through Maryland. Some citizens
hacked telegraph lines and cut down telegraph poles
to D.C. As a result, Maryland, which borders the
District of Columbia on three sides, was put under
martial law. The riot/massacre occurred eighty-six
years to the day after the first fight in the American
Revolution: the Battle of Lexington and Concord.

ABOVE J. Sella Martin, pastor of Boston's Joy Street Baptist Church. Martin was born in slavery in Charlotte, North Carolina. When he was a boy, he was sold apart from his mother and sister. He was sold several more times before escaping to the North in the 1850s, when he was in his early twenties.

OPPOSITE *Contraband of War*, from *A Popular History of the United States* (vol. 4, 1881). Seated at left: General Benjamin Butler. Standing in front of the table are presumably the three black men who took refuge at Fort Monroe in late May 1861: Frank Baker, Shepard Mallory, and James Townsend.

ARE NOT THESE *Northern people the most arrant cowards, as well as the biggest fools on earth? Just think of [Lieutenant Colonel Dimick] and [Lieutenant] Slemmer [at Fort Pickens, in Pensacola, Florida] sending back the fugitives that sought protection. . . . They refuse to let white men sell the Southerners food, and yet they return slaves to work on the plantation to raise all the food that the Southerners want.*

—J. Sella Martin to Frederick Douglass in a May 1861 letter, printed in the June 1861 issue of *Douglass' Monthly*

After the outbreak of the war, people who wanted to link preservation of the Union with black liberty had cause to both hurrah and hiss over actions taken by generals, by the Republican-dominated Congress, and by President Lincoln himself.

In May 1861, the Union's General Benjamin Franklin Butler, not an abolitionist, flouted the Fugitive Slave Law in his domain. This was the Virginia peninsula's Fort Monroe, where three black men sought sanctuary on May 23. When their owner, a Confederate colonel, got wind of their whereabouts, he requested their return.

On one condition, replied General Butler: that the colonel pledge allegiance to the USA. When the colonel refused, Butler kept the black men as contraband of war: that is, as confiscated enemy property of military value.

Butler wasn't in a quandary about what to do with the three black men. He put them to work. In justifying his actions to a superior, the general wrote: "I am credibly informed that the negroes in this neighborhood are now being employed in the erection of batteries and other works by the rebels, which it would be nearly or quite impossible to construct without their labor. Shall [the rebels] be allowed the use of this property against the United States, and we not be allowed its use in aid of the United States?"

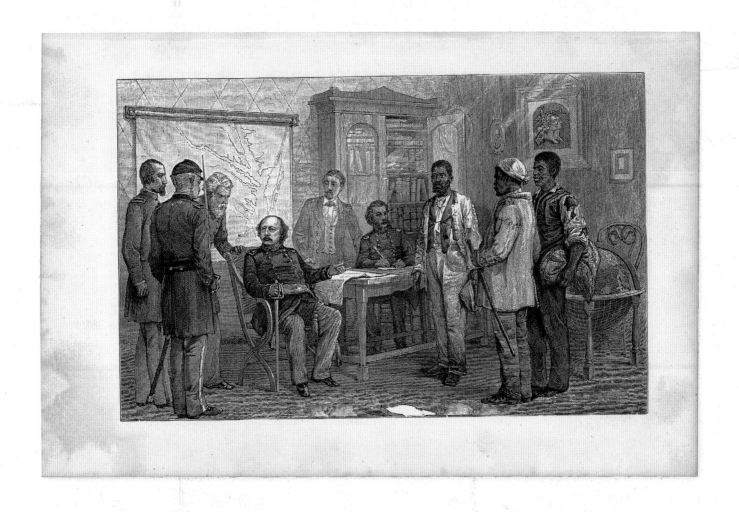

It wasn't long before droves of walking, talking "property" in the area headed to Butler's garrison, known on the grapevine as Freedom's Fort.

There were those in the Congress eager for the Union to be one great big "Freedom's Fort." While they held their fire on a state's right to slavery, most Republicans were ready to take aim at the property rights of *individuals* in rebellion—just as General Butler had done. They were all the more determined after July 21, 1861. This was the day of the CSA victory in the first major land battle: at Bull Run Creek near Manassas, Virginia, about twenty-five miles from Washington, D.C.

OPPOSITE *Secession Exploded* (1861), by William Wiswell. This cartoon casts secession as a monster and the Confederate states as equally vile. The artist also remarked on Southern states still in the Union. For example, Maryland (tugging on Uncle Sam's coattails) is portrayed as two-faced. Other states are two-headed, reflecting the existence of pro-Union and pro-Confederate factions within them.

ABOVE *Stampede of Slaves from Hampton to Fortress Monroe*, from the August 17, 1861, issue of *Harper's Weekly*. By early August 1861, roughly nine hundred black adults and children had made their way to "Freedom's Fort."

The Battle of Bull Run, also known as the Battle of Manassas. Of the estimated 32,000 Confederate troops who fought in this battle, there were some 1,700 casualties. Of the roughly 28,000 Union troops, there were about 3,000 casualties. The engraving from which this print was made originally appeared in the August 3, 1861, issue of *Frank Leslie's Illustrated Newspaper*.

Wild talk about Confederate atrocities against Union soldiers in the Battle of Bull Run—along with reports of Confederate use of slave labor during it—had hordes of Union loyalists hot for revenge.

So it was with significant support from the pro-Union public that, on August 6, 1861, Congress passed a bill introduced by Senator Lyman Trumbull, Republican of Illinois: "An Act to confiscate Property used for Insurrectionary Purposes." This bill sanctioned seizure of property used to aid the rebellion, whether weapons or wagons, plantations or people.

The "contrabands," as seized people were callously called, would enter a legal limbo. Technically, they would not be free but, rather, in the Union's custody.

Lincoln signed the confiscation bill into law, though it was bound to prompt squawks from many folks in the "border states," as slave states that had not joined the CSA were known: Delaware, Kentucky, Maryland, Missouri, and, though not a state, the federation of Virginia's western counties that remained loyal to the Union.

Within weeks of signing the Confiscation Act, Lincoln had something more explosive to worry about when it came to the border states.

THE FLASHPOINT WAS MISSOURI, WHERE CONFEDERATE sympathizers were engaging in guerrilla warfare and where CSA forces had gained some control of the southwestern part of the state.

The Union's man in charge of keeping Missouri in line was the former Republican presidential candidate, John Charles Frémont, now a general.

On August 30, 1861, from his base in St. Louis, Frémont put Missouri under martial law. In outlining what it meant to be under military rule, he proclaimed that, among other things, Confederate sympathizers would have their property seized. If that property included people, they would be *freed*!

Whoa!

Lincoln, who learned of Frémont's decree in the newspaper, couldn't let that stand. He promptly wrote to Frémont, pressing him to void the passage on freedom. Confiscation was fine, but freedom was political dynamite. It would, said Lincoln, "alarm our Southern Union friends, and turn them against us—perhaps ruin our rather fair prospect for Kentucky." Lincoln worried about Kentucky for good reason.

Back in April, when the president called out to the states for troops to put down the rebellion, his birth state had refused. Its governor, Beriah Magoffin, responded thusly: "I say, *emphatically*, Kentucky will furnish no troops for the wicked purpose of subduing her sister Southern states." Then, within weeks, Kentucky officially declared neutrality.

If Kentucky went over to the CSA, the Union would lose a major source of grain and livestock as well as open access to critical waterways, most especially the Ohio River. Lincoln feared that if Kentucky bolted, so might Missouri, also rich in resources. What's more, its largest city, St. Louis, was on the Mississippi River, key for transporting troops, supplies, and commercial goods, just like the Ohio River.

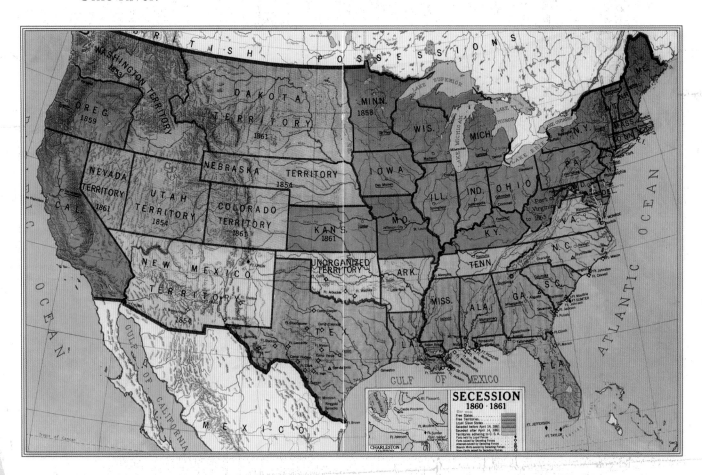

Secession, 1860–1861. Since 1854, several territories had been subdivided into new territories, and several states had entered the Union. *Purple*: free-soil states on the side of the Union. *Olive*: slave states that did not secede. *Pink*: pro-Union territories. *Dark orange*: slave states that seceded before the outbreak of war. *Light orange*: states that seceded after the outbreak of war. *Yellow*: territories that sided with the CSA, among them Indian Territory and the attached panhandle known as No Man's Land.

To his Excellency the President of the United States:

I feel it my duty to say that Major General Frémont's Proclamation, followed as it has been by the act of a military commission, manumitting slaves, is producing most disastrous results in this state, and that it is the opinion of many of our wisest and soundest men that if this is not immediately disavowed and annulled, Kentucky will be lost to the Union. I have already heard that on the reception of the news from Missouri, this morning a company which was ready to be sworn into the service was disbanded. Kentucky feels a direct interest in this matter, as a portion of General Frémont's force is now upon her soil.

Robert Anderson.

Louisville. Ky.
Sept. 13. 1861.

Letter from Gen. Robert Anderson to President Abraham Lincoln, September 13, 1861. Anderson, former commander of Fort Sumter, was now head of the Department of the Cumberland (Kentucky and Tennessee). In this letter, Anderson tells the president that Frémont's declaration of freedom is "producing most disastrous results" in Kentucky and could cause the state to leave the Union if not revoked. The letter is dated two days after Lincoln did just that, apparently unbeknownst to General Anderson.

After Frémont refused to revise his proclamation, Lincoln did it for him. (Their relationship was beyond repair. Before the year was out, the general was relieved of command.)

Many Union loyalists cheered Lincoln for revoking Frémont's freedom edict. But not abolitionists. They bombarded the president with letters of protest, pilloried him in publications, and commiserated with one another over what they saw as his maddening timidity.

"We cannot conquer the rebels as the war is now conducted," complained Republican Senator Charles Sumner to a friend. "There will be a vain masquerade of battles, a flux of blood and treasure, and nothing done!" What a shame, the senator lamented of Lincoln, "to have the power of a god and not to use it godlike!" Sumner, who was quite chummy with the president, had been urging him to declare immediate emancipation since the war began.

FRÉMONT'S PROCLAMATION HAS *in it that genuine military ring, that martial directness, for which the heart of the people in disturbed times always longs. They long for the man without fear—whose sword divides all meshes of compromise, all fine-spun legal doubts and hesitancies.*

—Harriet Beecher Stowe in *The Liberator* (September 20, 1861)

Harriet Beecher Stowe (ca. 1865). Stowe's bestseller, *Uncle Tom's Cabin* (1852), a sentimental novel about the horrors of slavery, brought countless people into the antislavery fold. It also earned its author, a native New Englander, the everlasting enmity of proslavery people.

"I think Sumner, and the rest of you, would upset our apple-cart altogether, if you had your way." That's what the cleric Charles Edwards Lester recalled Lincoln telling him. "We didn't go into the war to put *down* slavery, but to put the flag *back*." But the president didn't rule out a major move against slavery. "We must wait until every other means has been exhausted," Lincoln told Lester. *"This thunderbolt will keep."*

But wouldn't slavery enable the CSA to keep fighting?

"Camp of 'contrabands' of 13th" was written below this photograph, one of several on an album page devoted to the Thirteenth Massachusetts Infantry in Williamsport, Maryland, during the winter of 1861–62. Almost always, blacks who took refuge with Union soldiers worked for their keep. Their duties ranged from cooking and doing laundry to digging trenches and serving as scouts.

Of the nation's roughly four million people in bondage, about 3.5 million of them were in the Confederate states. Even if toddlers and old folks were subtracted from that number, that still left a lot of forced laborers at the CSA's disposal.

These black people didn't just raise cotton and food crops. They didn't just build batteries. They were also cooks and coopers, bakers, butchers, blacksmiths, and boatmen. And some were put to work in weapon-making factories and shops, such as the one at Tredegar Iron Works in Richmond, Virginia, capital of the Confederacy.

All this black labor freed up whites for combat. Plus, people in bondage had information the Union could use (on troop movements, for example). Letting the CSA keep such a valuable resource was insane, charged abolitionists.

Abolitionists had more to deplore in Lincoln's Annual Message to Congress, in December 1861. In it, the president proposed freedom for the so-called contrabands—referring to them, oddly, as having been "liberated" by the Confiscation Act. The freedom he now broached had a string attached. Congress would have to earmark money for sending "contrabands" out of the country.

And not just them.

"It might be well to consider, too," added Lincoln, "whether the free colored people already in the United States could not, so far as individuals may desire, be included in such colonization."

Lincoln, a member of the Illinois Colonization Society in the 1850s, couldn't see blacks ever getting a fair shake in America, nor could he envision blacks and whites living together in peace.

Plenty of whites outside the CSA felt the same way. The nation's roughly 500,000 free blacks faced intense discrimination at almost every turn: barred from certain schools, banned from certain jobs, denied the right to vote in some localities. What's more, in some states, including Lincoln's Illinois, it was a crime for blacks to take up residence there.

For many whites in Illinois and elsewhere in the North and West, the idea of millions of freed blacks was a frightful thing. Some feared that blacks would seek bloody revenge against whites in the South. Others feared that freed people

---

EMANCIPATION LEAGUE.

DECLARATION.

The object of this League is to urge upon the People and the Government EMANCIPATION OF THE SLAVES, as a measure of justice, and as a military necessity ; it being the shortest, cheapest, and least bloody path to permanent peace, and the only method of maintaining the integrity of the nation.

ARTICLE 1. Any person who signs this Constitution and contributes to the funds of the League shall be a member, and by payment of five dollars shall be a Life-Member, exempt from further payments.

ARTICLE 2. The officers shall be a President, Vice-President, Secretary, and Treasurer, who, with a Committee of seven, shall constitute an Executive Board,—all to be elected at the Annual Meeting, and to hold until their successors are elected. They shall perform the duties usually pertaining to those offices, and no one except the Secretary shall be paid for his services.

ARTICLE 3. The Annual Meeting shall be fixed by the Executive Board.

ARTICLE 4. The Executive Board shall meet at least once in each month, and as much oftener as they may deem necessary. They shall expend the funds of the League for the promotion of its object, by publications, lectures, circulars, petitions to Congress, or by such other means as they may deem proper and useful, and they shall render an annual account of their doings and expenses.

ARTICLE 5. The Treasurer shall have custody of all the funds of the League. He shall pay nothing except upon the written order of the Executive Board, and he shall annually render an account of his receipts and disbursements.

ARTICLE 6. Branch Leagues may be organized under such regulations as the Executive Board may authorize.

ADOPTED AT BOSTON, Nov. 19, 1861.

Declaration, 1861. Formed to push the public—and Lincoln—to hit hard at slavery, the Emancipation League championed abolition "as a measure of justice and as a military necessity." Frederick Douglass and Wendell Phillips lectured for the league. Its chief financial backer was George Stearns, a wealthy white manufacturer. Other white members included Julia Ward Howe and her husband, physician Samuel Gridley Howe. Howe and Stearns had been members of the Secret Six, the group that had financed John Brown.

would troop north and west seeking even freer air. And this fear spawned other phantom fears: that blacks wouldn't be able to function in freedom and thus would become burdens; that blacks *would* be able to function in freedom and thus threaten white jobs.

There were also whites who had no fear but simply didn't want throngs of blacks in their midst. This was akin to some whites opposing slavery in the territories: they wanted the territories to be lands of opportunity—not for already wealthy slave-holding planters but for workaday whites, allowing them the chance at what would later be known as the American Dream.

Republican senator Henry Wilson of Massachusetts (ca. 1860–65), a future vice president under president Ulysses S. Grant.

So Lincoln was hardly alone in favoring colonization. Not in the 1850s and not during the Civil War. In the summer of 1861, Republican Senator James Henry Lane, a champion of a free-soil Kansas, had called for blacks and whites to be kept apart. Far apart—as in "an ocean rolling between them." Lane envisioned South America an ideal place for blacks, or as he put it, "the elysium of the colored man." America would be "the elysium of the white."

WHILE CONGRESS CHEWED ON LINCOLN'S PITCH FOR colonization funds in December 1861, it was dealing with an antislavery bill introduced by Senator Henry Wilson of Massachusetts. His bill called for immediate emancipation where the federal government had undisputed jurisdiction: Washington, D.C.

In was also in December 1861 that Secretary of War Simon Cameron created a stir with his annual report, for in it he recommended that the Union Army use "contrabands" in combat. Worse, the report was leaked to the press. Lincoln was not happy. It was yet another idea to horrify many white loyalists, especially in the border states, two of which were embroiled in their own civil wars.

In October, a pro-Confederate faction of Missouri's legislature had established its own government, in Neosho, on the Arkansas-Missouri border. In November, the same thing had happened in Kentucky. There, the pro-Confederate government claimed Bowling Green as its capital. These developments made Secretary of War Cameron's proposal to arm blacks who escaped to Union lines—many of them from the border states—like adding fuel to a fire.

Cameron, already under scrutiny for corruption, wouldn't be issuing any more potentially rebel-rousing reports. Lincoln made sure that there was an ocean rolling between Cameron and the nation: In January 1862, the president made him ambassador to Russia.

By then, the rump governments of Kentucky and Missouri had been admitted into the CSA.

AND THE WAR RAGED ON. UNION AND CONFEDERATE FORCES continued the wounding and the killing in skirmishes and full-blown battles, gunning for each other on land, at sea, in swamps, from trees—and the CSA was far from being licked.

Abolitionists clamored all the louder for Lincoln to champion black liberty as key to Union victory.

SLAVERY IS THE *stomach of the rebellion. The bread that feeds the rebel army, the cotton that clothes them, and the money that arms them and keeps them supplied with powder and bullets, come from the slaves. . . . Strike here . . . and you at once put an end to this rebellion. . . . Shall this not be done, because we shall offend the Union men in the border states?*

—Frederick Douglass in *Douglass' Monthly*
(September 1861)

In a January 1862 speech in the House of Representatives, Pennsylvania's Thaddeus Stevens called emancipation "the most terrible weapon" in the Union's armory. "Universal emancipation must be proclaimed to all," he said. Stevens had long believed that emancipation was a moral necessity. Now, along with seeing it as a weapon, he thought it essential for a permanent peace between North and South.

Slavery was the cause of the war, Stevens insisted. Even if the Union won it, if the nation did not eradicate slavery, war would come again, he predicted. Stevens thus urged: "While you are quelling this insurrection at such fearful cost, remove the cause, that future generations may live in peace."

Republican representative Thaddeus Stevens of Pennsylvania (ca.1861).

THEY MAY SEND *the flower of their young men down South . . . one year, two years, three years, till they are tired of sending, or till they use up all the young men. All no use! God's ahead of Master Lincoln. God will [not let] Master Lincoln beat the South till he do the right thing.*

—Harriet Tubman (according to abolitionist Lydia Maria Child in a January 1862 letter to poet John Greenleaf Whittier, another abolitionist)

On the face of it, the president wasn't persuaded by Stevens or anyone else to strike hard at slavery. But he revealed himself ready to chip away at it.

On March 6, 1862, Lincoln asked Congress to back compensated, gradual emancipation. Specifically, he wanted the senators and representatives to issue the following joint resolution:

RESOLVED:

That the United States ought to cooperate with any State which may adopt gradual abolishment of slavery, giving to such State [financial] aid, to be used by such State in its discretion, to compensate for the inconveniences, public and private, produced by such change of system.

Lincoln long believed that the most peaceable, practical way to end slavery in the states was for the U.S. government to pay them to phase it out, as some Northern states had done (but without compensation). For example, Pennsylvania's gradual emancipation act had set a time frame for the freedom of children born to enslaved women after March 1, 1780, the date of the act's passage. These children were to be indentured servants until age twenty-eight, then free.

THE LATE MESSAGE *of President Lincoln to Congress, relative to emancipation, has given rise to more speculations, and created more surmises than any other document ever issued from the mansion halls of the White House. . . .*

I look at it as one of the most ingenious subterfuges. . . . [I]t denies that Congress has any power to legislate on slavery—leaving it under the absolute control of individual States.

—Henry McNeal Turner in *The Christian Recorder* (March 22, 1862)

While Lincoln waited for that yes or no on the joint resolution on compensated, gradual emancipation, Congress passed, in early March, and the president approved, a measure that Senator Charles Sumner had championed: an additional article of war that forbade Union officers to return "fugitives from service or labor" to their owners. This article of war gutted the 1850 Fugitive Slave Law.

Was the Union becoming one great big "Freedom's Fort" after all? Would the border states see the writing on the wall and say yes to compensated, gradual emancipation? Or would they stand firm for slavery?

While the world awaited the outcome, more enslaved people made a dash for freedom. Still others, staying put, engaged in sabotage, from work slowdowns to torching Confederate property: military, municipal, and civilian.

In the meantime, the border states seemed less of a worry to many people loyal to the Union. By late March 1862, it was highly unlikely that Maryland and Delaware would go over to the CSA. Yes, pro-Confederate sympathies remained strong in these states, but so too was the presence of Union troops. Also by then, the Union had routed CSA forces from southwestern Missouri.

As for Kentucky, the Union didn't yet have a total lock on that state, but in February, its forces had taken Bowling Green, capital of the Confederate shadow government.

COMPENSATED, GRADUAL EMANCIPATION WAS SOON IN THE news again. On April 10, 1862, Congress gave the president that joint resolution he wanted.

Two days later, a bill that abolitionists wanted to clear Congress did: the one making the District of Columbia slavery-free.

As Lincoln wished, the bill included compensation to slaveholders loyal to the Union. For loss of their human property, the U.S. government would pay them up to three hundred dollars per person on average. The people freed, along with blacks in D.C. already free, would receive one hundred dollars, but only if they moved to Haiti, Liberia, or another nation of the president's choosing.

Most abolitionists couldn't stomach slaveholders getting even a cent and despised Lincoln's push for colonization. Yet they had to let out a huge "Hallelujah!" after the president signed the D.C. Emancipation Act into law on April 16. Roughly three thousand blacks were now forever free. (How many of them accepted the hundred dollars and left the country is unknown, but on April 21, Congress received a petition from forty blacks in D.C. seeking help in emigrating to Central America. Two days later there was a similar petition from twenty. Henry McNeal Turner was among the signers.)

Petition for owner compensation (page one). Former slaveholder John Harry of Georgetown filed for compensation on April 29, 1862. He claimed a loss of twenty-seven people because of the D.C. Emancipation Act. They included Grace Butler (about fifty-eight years old), her two daughters Martha and Eliza Ann (about thirty-four and twenty), and her son Walter (sixteen). Harry stated that the mother was of "strong frame," and complained of rheumatism. He valued her at one hundred dollars (but the government valued her at $43.80). All told, the U.S. government paid more than nine hundred D.C. slaveholders close to one million dollars for black people they had held in slavery.

PETITION.

To the Commissioners under the act of Congress approved the 16th of April, 1862,
entitled "An act for the release of certain persons held to service or labor in the
District of Columbia."

Your Petitioner, *John Hovay* — of *George Town D.C.*,
by this *his* petition in writing, represents and states, that *he* is a person loyal to the
United States, who, at the time of the passage of the said act of Congress, held a claim to
service or labor against *the Twenty seven*
person of African descent of the name of *Grace Butler and others*
whose names, ages, value and description are
hereunto annexed

for and during the life of said *Twenty seven Slaves*
and that by said act of Congress said ~~slaves~~ *Slaves were* ~~was~~ discharged and
freed of and from all claim of your petitioner to such service or labor; that at the time of said
discharge said *Twenty seven Slaves, were* ~~was~~ of the age of ―
and of the personal description following: [1] *Viz:*

~~Grace Butler~~ Slave, aged about 5[?] years Black
strong frame, complains of Rheumatism £ 100.00 *value*
Martha her daughter about 34 years of age
Black, Slave good size, in good health ― 600.00
Eliza Ann Butler Graces daughter, slave
aged about 20 years, black in good health 800.00
Walter Butler, Graces son 16 years old Slave
small size black, in good health ― 880.00
Grace was presented to me by Mrs Martha
Clagett of George Town D.C, the Mother of my
first wife; when she, Grace was a small girl
and resided in my family until three or four
years since, her three children above named
were born in my house ―
Jane Coney aged about 37 years, in good health
black, small stature was born in my
house of a slave woman ― 550.00
Lydia Meredith aged about 43 years, Mulatto
slave in good health ― 500.00
Richard Meredith about 25 years old Slave
dark Mulatto about 5 feet 7 or 8 Inches high
in good health ― 1200.00
John Meredith aged 23 years dark Mulatto

In 1862, blacks in Washington, D.C., certainly celebrated the end of slavery in the nation's capital, but they didn't have their first grand Emancipation Parade until after the war, as depicted here in F. Dielman's *Celebration of the Abolition of Slavery in the District of Columbia by the Colored People, in Washington, April 19, 1866*. His engraving originally appeared in the May 12, 1866, issue of *Harper's Weekly*.

Republican representative Owen
Lovejoy of Illinois (ca. 1850–60).

BANNING SLAVERY IN THE TERRI-tories was still on the Republican agenda. In early May 1862, an Illinois representative launched his crusade in Congress for a bill doing just this. He was Owen Lovejoy, a younger brother of the abolition-ist Elijah Lovejoy, murdered by a proslavery mob twenty-five years earlier.

As with other antislavery measures, forbidding slavery in the territories would be easier now that the war was on. Many Democrats who would have fought tooth and nail to kill such a bill had gone over to the CSA. (At the time, there were few enslaved people in the territories. According to the 1860 census, Utah, for example, had twenty-nine.)

WHAT I BELIEVE *is this: we have opened in our national history the chapter which is to record the freedom of every man under the stars and stripes. Abraham Lincoln may not wish it; he cannot prevent it; the nation may not will it, but the nation can never prevent it. . . . For the first time in our history for seventy years, the government, as a corporation, has spoken antislavery words and done antislavery deeds. It is a momentous alteration in the heart that governs the government. I allude to that fact, not because I care for the state of mind of Mr. Lincoln or the Cabinet specifically; I view them as milestones.*

—Wendell Phillips on May 6, 1862, at the
American Anti-Slavery Society's 29th annual convention, in New York City

Freedom seemed fast on the march down south, following Union victories in coastal South Carolina, Georgia, and Florida. On May 9, the Union's General David Hunter put these states under martial law. What's more, Hunter declared that everyone held in captivity in those states was *free*.

Just as with Frémont's freedom decree, Lincoln quashed Hunter's. In a proclamation on May 19, the president stressed that *no one* had been authorized to declare *anyone* free in *any* state.

> **THE SOUTH, HAVING** *been deceived in regard to Mr. Lincoln and the aims of the Republican party, went to war to protect slavery. Now, perhaps, they are beginning to see that Mr. Lincoln is not so far from a slave-catcher, after all.*
>
> —Anna E. Dickinson, furious over the Hunter affair, at the annual New England Anti-Slavery Convention on May 28, 1862, in Boston

Interestingly, Lincoln followed this pronouncement, so pleasing to proslavery activists, with words apt to make some abolitionists take heart: If a major emancipation edict became "a necessity" to save the Union, then that was *his* call as commander in chief of the U.S. armed forces.

In this proclamation the president also urged slaveholding states to say yes to compensated, gradual emancipation. This was not his first appeal.

Philadelphia-born Anna E. Dickinson (ca. 1861–65). In January 1860, seventeen-year-old Dickinson made her debut as a public speaker with some impromptu remarks at a program called "Woman's Rights and Wrongs." That fall she spoke out against slavery at the Pennsylvania Anti-Slavery Society's annual meeting. Thanks to William Lloyd Garrison, Dickinson was soon giving speeches around New England.

Back in late 1861, Lincoln had secretly tried and failed to get a yes from the legislature of Delaware, a state with fewer than two thousand people in slavery (not even 2 percent of the population).

After Lincoln's May 1862 appeal, Delaware still didn't bite. Neither did any other state. Not in May. And not after June 19—the day the bill prohibiting slavery in the territories, having cleared Congress, was sent to Lincoln.

He signed it into law straightaway.

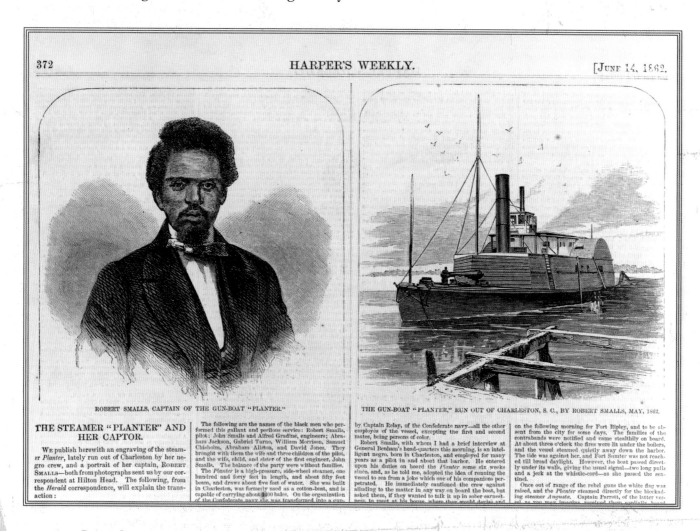

372   HARPER'S WEEKLY.   [JUNE 14, 1862.

ROBERT SMALLS, CAPTAIN OF THE GUN-BOAT "PLANTER."

THE GUN-BOAT "PLANTER," RUN OUT OF CHARLESTON, S. C., BY ROBERT SMALLS, MAY, 1862.

THE STEAMER "PLANTER" AND HER CAPTOR.

WE publish herewith an engraving of the steamer *Planter*, lately run out of Charleston by her negro crew, and a portrait of her captain, ROBERT SMALLS—both from photographs sent us by our correspondent at Hilton Head. The following, from the *Herald* correspondence, will explain the transaction:

The following are the names of the black men who performed this gallant and perilous service: Robert Smalls, pilot; John Smalls and Alfred Gradine, engineers; Abraham Jackson, Gabriel Turno, William Morrison, Samuel Chisholm, Abraham Allston, and David Jones. They brought with them the wife and three children of the pilot, and the wife, child, and sister of the first engineer, John Smalls. The balance of the party were without families.

The *Planter* is a high-pressure, side-wheel steamer, one hundred and forty feet in length, and about fifty feet beam, and draws about five feet of water. She was built in Charleston, was formerly used as a cotton-boat, and is capable of carrying about 1400 bales. On the organization of the Confederate navy she was transformed into a gun-

boat, by Captain Relay, of the Confederate navy—all the other employés of the vessel, excepting the first and second mates, being persons of color.

Robert Smalls, with whom I had a brief interview at General Benham's head-quarters this morning, is an intelligent negro, born in Charleston, and employed for many years as a pilot in and about that harbor. He entered upon his duties on board the *Planter* some six weeks since, and, as he told me, adopted the idea of running the vessel to sea from a joke which one of his companions perpetrated. He immediately cautioned the crew against alluding to the matter in any way on board the boat, but asked them, if they wanted to talk it up in sober earnest, to meet at his house, where they would devise and

on the following morning for Fort Ripley, and to be absent from the city for some days. The families of the contrabands were notified and came stealthily on board. At about three o'clock the fires were lit under the boilers, and the vessel steamed quietly away down the harbor. The tide was against her, and Fort Sumter was not reached till broad daylight. However, the boat passed directly under its walls, giving the usual signal—two long pulls and a jerk at the whistle-cord—as she passed the sentinel.

Once out of range of the rebel guns the white flag was raised, and the *Planter* steamed directly for the blockading steamer *Augusta*. Captain Parrott, of the latter vessel, as you may imagine, received them cordially, heard

Robert Smalls was on the lookout for a chance to escape slavery since the start of the war. He took his liberty in May 1862 aboard the CSA gunboat *Planter*, piloting the vessel out of Charleston Harbor. His family and about a dozen other enslaved adults and children were with him.

SLAVERY, LONG OUTLAWED IN THE NORTH, WAS NOW OUT-
lawed in the District of Columbia and in the territories. More people in captivity
in the CSA and in the border states were taking their liberty, making the most
of the chaos of war, a war in its second year. Still, Lincoln gave no signal that
he deemed a major freedom decree "a necessity." The president kept everybody
guessing.

On the Fourth of July 1862, Charles Sumner begged Lincoln to strike hard
at slavery and thereby make the day "more sacred and more historic." Said
Sumner: "You need more men, not only at the North, but at the South, in the
rear of the rebels; you need the slaves."

"Too big a lick," Lincoln replied. He projected that half the Union troops
would desert in protest. He also expressed concern about the border states.

A week later, the president met with representatives of the border states. In
urging them to say yes to compensated, gradual emancipation, Lincoln tried
some of everything.

He appealed to their patriotism, arguing that a yes would be a powerful show
of support for the Union, strong enough to take the wind out of the CSA's sails.
It would shorten the war.

He appealed to their wallets, maintaining that if the war dragged on, slavery
"will be gone, and you will have nothing valuable in lieu of it."

He also appealed to their prejudice: "When numbers shall be large enough
to be company and encouragement for one another, the freed people will not be
so reluctant to go [to voluntarily leave the country]."

Two days later, on July 14, Lincoln received a letter with the majority decision: no. They wouldn't let slavery go.

As for their support of the Union, these border state representatives assured

Lincoln that he could count on that, but it wasn't unconditional. "Confine yourself to your constitutional authority," they wrote. "Confine your subordinates within the same limits; conduct this war solely for the purpose of restoring the Constitution to its legitimate authority; concede to each state and its loyal citizens, their just rights, and we are wedded to you by indissoluble ties."

While the border states stood their ground, on July 17, Congress passed and Lincoln signed two bills advancing liberty.

There was the Militia Act. It authorized Lincoln to let blacks serve in the U.S. armed forces as laborers and in any other capacity "for which they may be found competent." In the case of black boys and men who belonged to Confederates, they would be declared free, along with their mothers, wives, and children (if they, too, had Confederate owners).

Republican senator Lyman Trumbull of Illinois (ca. 1861).

Mightier than the Militia Act was the second Confiscation Act. Like the first, its "father" was Senator Lyman Trumbull.

Under this new bill, the property of anyone who in any way supported the CSA could be seized. When it came to human property, whether they escaped, were captured in battle, or were abandoned, these people wouldn't be left in legal limbo. They would be "forever free of their servitude and not again held as slaves."

This confiscation act applied imme-

diately to leading members of the CSA, such as its president and other government officials. For less prominent supporters of the rebellion, the president had to first issue a public warning giving them sixty days to return their allegiance to the Union or risk seizure of their property.

The second Confiscation Act also reinforced part of the Militia Act by empowering the president to "employ as many persons of African descent as he may deem necessary and proper" for quashing the rebellion.

What's more, the second Confiscation Act scratched Lincoln's itch for colonization. It gave him broad powers to move blacks to "some tropical country." But there were conditions: blacks had to be willing to go, and this country had to be willing to receive them "with all the rights and privileges of freemen." Lincoln also had a big budget for colonization. Months back, tied to the D.C. Emancipation Act, Congress had appropriated one hundred thousand dollars for colonization. On July 16, 1862, the day before passage of the second Confiscation Act, Congress approved a spending bill that earmarked for colonization another five hundred thousand dollars (roughly eleven million dollars today).

<hr>

THE TROPICAL CLIME UPPERMOST ON THE PRESIDENT'S mind for blacks was the province of Chiriquí in present-day Panama. Back in 1861, Lincoln had been much persuaded by the claims of shipping magnate Ambrose Thompson, chief of the Chiriquí Improvement Company. According to Thompson, his firm owned several hundred thousand acres of land in Chiriquí, where blacks from America, the thinking went, could build new lives for themselves as farmers (growing coffee, cotton, rice, and other crops) or as coal miners given the purported rich deposits of that ore.

On August 14, 1862, Lincoln met in the White House with five men of some mark in D.C.'s black community. It was a delegation headed by Edward M. Thomas, president of the Anglo-African Institute for the Encouragement of Industry and Art. Lincoln wanted these men to recruit a band of blacks (ideally, groups of families) for a pilot emigration program.

"You and we are different races," the president told the delegation. "We have between us a broader difference than exists between almost any other two races. Whether it is right or wrong I need not discuss, but this physical difference is a great disadvantage to us both, as I think your race suffer very greatly, many of them by living among us, while ours suffer from your presence."

Solution: separation of the races.

Calling slavery "the greatest wrong inflicted on any people," Lincoln stated that even when blacks "cease to be slaves, you are yet far removed from being placed on an equality with the white race."

And it was a white race shedding rivers of its own blood: "See our present condition—the country engaged in war!—our white men cutting one another's throats, none knowing how far it will extend; and then consider what we know to be the truth. But for your race among us there could be no war."

The president's remarks, reported by the press, earned him praise from negrophobes. The *New York Herald,* for one, beamed over the "great truth" Lincoln had spoken about the races, though not over his plans for colonization, thinking it not feasible. The nation needed the labor, the newspaper argued, favoring "the mild servitude of the Southern states" for blacks. As for abolitionists, "squelch them," said the *Herald,* insisting that abolitionists, by their agitation over the last thirty years, had "caused the war."

Not surprisingly, what Lincoln said to that black delegation enraged more than a few abolitionists, some of whom called for *slaveholders* to be colonized beyond the nation's shores.

OPPOSITE *Political Caricature. No. 4, The Miscegenation Ball* (1864) by Kimmel & Foster. This lithograph lampoons the Republican Party as infatuated with black people. Like other cartoons of the era, it alludes to one reason why many whites opposed emancipation and advocated separation of the races: fear that freedom would lead to widespread race mixing, also known as "miscegenation." This would, in turn, lead to romances and ultimately to the "mongrelization" of the white race. Ironically, many people who opposed voluntary interracial relationships never had a problem with the fact that many enslaved black women were forced to have relations with white men, as happened to the mothers of Frederick Douglass and J. Sella Martin.

LEFT Frances E. W. Harper, from *The Underground Railroad* (1872), by her friend William Still. Harper, a writer, teacher, and Underground Railroad aide, was born free in a slave state (Maryland). Although she curtailed her lecturing in 1860 when she married Fenton Harper of Ohio, she made her anti-colonization stance known through her writing.

A SPECTACLE, AS *humiliating as it was extraordinary, was presented to all Christendom on the afternoon of the 14th. . . . By special invitation of President Lincoln, a committee of the colored people . . . appeared before him, to listen to a proposition, on his part, for their removal to Central America. . . . Can anything be more puerile, absurd, illogical, impertinent, untimely?*

—William Lloyd Garrison in *The Liberator* (August 22, 1862)

NO, MR. PRESIDENT, *it is not the innocent horse that makes the horse thief, not the traveler's purse that makes the highway robber, and it is not the presence of the negro that causes this foul and unnatural war, but the cruel and brutal cupidity of those who wish to possess horses, money and negroes by means of theft, robbery, and rebellion.*

—Frederick Douglass in *Douglass' Monthly* (September 1862)

LET THE PRESIDENT *be answered firmly and respectfully . . . that while we admit the right of every man to choose his home, that we neither see the wisdom nor expediency of our self-exportation from a land which has been in a measure enriched by our toil for generations.*

—Frances E. W. Harper in *The Christian Recorder* (September 27, 1862)

The best-known public rebuke Lincoln received on the matter of slavery came from Horace Greeley, the editor of the widely read *New-York Daily Tribune*. On August 19, Greeley wrote Lincoln a fever-pitch letter. The next day Greeley published it in his newspaper under the headline THE PRAYER OF THE TWENTY MILLIONS (as if he were speaking for every soul in the North).

Millions of Americans, said Greeley, were "sorely disappointed and deeply pained by the policy you seem to be pursuing with regard to the slaves of the rebels." Forget about the "fossil politicians" in the border states, said Greeley. Hurl a thunderbolt at slavery. "On the face of this wide earth,

Horace Greeley from Amherst, New Hampshire (ca. 1862).

Mr. President, there is not one disinterested, determined, intelligent champion of the Union cause who does not feel that all attempts to put down the rebellion and at the same time uphold its inciting cause [slavery] are preposterous and futile—that the rebellion, if crushed out tomorrow, would be renewed within a year if slavery were left in full vigor."

Three days later, Lincoln's response to Greeley—in full vigor—appeared in the *Daily National Intelligencer*, a D.C. newspaper:

My paramount object in this struggle *is* to save the Union, and is *not* either to save or to destroy slavery. If I could save the Union without freeing *any* slave, I would do it, and if I could save it by freeing *all* the slaves I would do it; and if I could save it by freeing some and leaving others alone I would also do that. What I do about slavery, and the colored race, I do because I believe it helps to save the Union; and what I forbear, I forbear because I do *not* believe it would help to save the Union.

Lincoln didn't end on a fire-breathing note. He sounded apologetic. "I have here stated my purpose according to my view of *official* duty, and I intend no modification of my oft-expressed *personal* wish that all men, everywhere could be free."

Yet again, the president gave proslavery *and* antislavery people something on which to pin their hopes. What was he thinking? If Lincoln left any personal notes on the matter, they have yet to see the light of day. His motives remain the subject of debate.

WAS HE CONFUSED? BEING SHREWD? AND WAS THIS letter, which Lincoln sent to that D.C. newspaper, in part about damage control? The day before Lincoln's letter to Greeley ran in the *Intelligencer*, Greeley's *Tribune* told its readers something Lincoln could hardly have wanted broadcast.

"In justice to all parties," announced the *Tribune* on August 22, "it seems proper to state the following, which we learn from so many sources that it can no longer be considered a state secret."

The newspaper reported that Lincoln had recently shared with his cabinet a proclamation of emancipation "abolishing slavery wherever on the 1st of next December the rebellion" had not been "crushed."

Of the seven cabinet members, one was absent, the *Tribune* believed. Of the six present, four gave the proclamation their blessing. However, Lincoln changed his mind about issuing it because the secretary of state, William Seward, and the postmaster general, Montgomery Blair, had "opposed it with all their might." Greeley's newspaper had a number of things wrong, but quite a few things right.

A month before, on July 22, Lincoln had indeed spoken with his cabinet, all seven members, about a proclamation on emancipation. It began with his reading his rough draft of a three-point decree.

1. Pursuant to the second Confiscation Act, he would warn all persons supporting the Confederacy (apart from specified Confederate leaders, whose property was already subject to seizure) that they risked having their property seized.
2. In pursuit of peace and restoration of the Union, the offer of compensation for gradual emancipation was still on the table.
3. "And, as a fit and necessary military measure," he, as commander in chief of the Union armed forces, would declare on January 1, 1863, people enslaved in Confederate territory "shall then, thenceforward, and forever, be free."

Lincoln was prepared to go public with his proclamation without delay.

As the *Tribune* had reported, Seward did oppose the proclamation. It wasn't because the secretary of state was anti-emancipation. It was the timing that

In pursuance of the sixth section of the act of congress entitled "An act to suppress insurrection and to punish treason and rebellion, to seize and confiscate property of rebels, and for other purposes" Approved July 17. 1862, and which act, and the joint Resolution explanatory thereof, are herewith published, I. Abraham Lincoln, President of the United States, do hereby proclaim to, and warn all persons within the contemplation of said sixth section to cease participating in, aiding, countenancing, or abetting the existing rebellion, or any rebellion against the government of the United States, and to return to their proper allegiance to the United States, on pain of the forfeitures and seizures, as within and by said sixth section provided—

And I hereby make known that it is my purpose, upon the next meeting of Congress, to again recommend the adoption of a practical measure for tendering pecuniary aid to the free choice or rejection, of any and all States, which may then be recognizing and practically sustaining the authority of the United States, and which may then have voluntarily adopted, or thereafter may voluntarily adopt, gradual abolishment of slavery within such State or States— that the object is to practically restore, thenceforward to be maintain, the constitutional relation between the general government, and each, and all the states, wherein that relation bothered him. The Union's General George B. McClellan had recently failed to capture Richmond in the Peninsula Campaign. If Lincoln issued the proclamation right then, the Union might appear weak, desperate, Seward feared. He thought it made more sense to announce the proclamation when the Union had something to crow about militarily.

Secretary of the Navy Gideon Welles didn't promote or protest the proclamation during the meeting, but he later wrote of having qualms about such an "extreme exercise of war powers."

Like Welles, Secretary of the Interior Caleb Smith, no fan of emancipation, kept his thoughts to himself during the meeting.

In contrast, Montgomery Blair, the postmaster general, spoke his mind. He feared that the proclamation would rile the border states. Blair also felt that it would make whites elsewhere in the Union howl. As a result, Republicans would pay dearly in the midterm elections in the coming fall.

is now suspended, or disturbed; and that, for this object, the war, as it has been, will be, prosecuted. And, as a fit and necessary military measure for effecting this object, I, as Commander-in-chief of the Army and Navy of the United States, do order and declare that on the first day of January in the year of our Lord one thousand, eight hundred and sixty three, all persons held as slaves within any state or states, wherein the constitutional authority of the United States shall not then be practically recognized, submitted to, and maintained, shall then, thenceforward, and forever, be free,

OPPOSITE AND LEFT Draft of the Emancipation Proclamation by President Abraham Lincoln, July 22, 1862. Lincoln shared this draft with his cabinet shortly after the border states said no to compensated, gradual emancipation.

First Reading of the Emancipation Proclamation of President Lincoln (1864), oil on canvas by Francis Bicknell Carpenter. Left to right: Stanton, Chase (*standing*), Lincoln, Welles, Smith, Seward (*seated in foreground*), Blair, and Bates. Details in the painting include a copy of the Constitution (*on the table between Lincoln and Seward*); a map of the slave population (*on the floor behind Bates*); and a copy of the *New-York Daily Tribune* (*far left, behind Stanton's chair*). The July 22 meeting was held, it is believed, in Lincoln's office, roughly the space the Lincoln Bedroom occupies today in the White House.

Secretary of the Treasury Salmon Chase, antislavery to the bone, supported the proclamation even though he opposed compensation for emancipation (as he did colonization). Also, Chase would have preferred something akin to a controlled demolition: let Union forces declare people forever free as they conquered land. In other words, let the second Confiscation Act do its work.

The man who had replaced Simon Cameron as secretary of war, Edwin Stanton, was in favor of Lincoln issuing his proclamation right away. Stanton believed in denying the CSA black labor as much as he believed in black liberty.

The remaining cabinet member, Attorney General Edward Bates, also had no problem with the proclamation (but at the time he did have a problem with Lincoln's insistence on *encouraging* blacks to emigrate. Bates was for straight-out deportation).

In the end, Lincoln decided to pocket his proclamation, to wait.

While Lincoln waited, on July 25 he issued a proclamation, authorized under the second Confiscation Act, warning rank-and-file Confederates that if they did not cease and desist from rebellion within sixty days, their property—including people enslaved—was in jeopardy of being seized.

While Lincoln waited, his emancipation edict was neither out of sight nor out of mind. He revised it. At one point, he added that "the effort to colonize persons of African descent upon this continent, or elsewhere will be continued." He also noted that he would recommend that at the end of the hostilities, people loyal to the Union be compensated for "all losses by acts of the United States, including the loss of slaves."

While Lincoln waited, he also gave Secretary of War Stanton a secret go-ahead on the matter of black troops. In turn, Stanton, also on the quiet, authorized General Rufus Saxton in South Carolina to raise a black fighting force of up to five thousand men.

Naturally, while Lincoln waited, he paid close attention to battlefield reports. More dead. More maimed. And no shining victory for the Union to claim. The bad news included Union defeat in the Second Battle of Bull Run.

But then came the combat near Sharpsburg, Maryland, by Antietam Creek. There, on September 17, 1862, the Confederate general Robert E. Lee found his troops greatly outnumbered in phase one of his plan to invade the North.

After a day of awful slaughter on both sides, the Battle of Antietam ended with CSA forces in retreat.

OUR ARMS VICTORIOUS, proclaimed the *Boston Evening Transcript* on September 19.

GREAT VICTORY, the *New York Times* boomed the next day.

Lincoln's wait ended two days later, on Monday, September 22, 1862. "I think the time has come now," Treasury Secretary Chase recalled the president telling his cabinet on this day, the day of the expiration of that warning Lincoln had given on July 25.

"I wish it were a better time," Lincoln continued. "I wish that we were in a better condition. The action of the army against the rebels has not been quite what I should have best liked. But they have been driven out of Maryland, and Pennsylvania is no longer in danger of invasion." He also said that at one point he promised himself and his "Maker" that if CSA troops were driven from Maryland, he would announce the Emancipation Proclamation.

To that end, the president then conferred with his cabinet on his latest draft of the document. After that, he went public with this decree. Lincoln put the Union, the Confederacy—the world—on notice that, come January 1, 1863, he would declare every captive black soul in CSA-controlled territory "forever free."

GOD BLESS ABRAHAM LINCOLN! blared Greeley's *Tribune* on September 23.

But the decree said (or implied) that if the Confederacy laid down its arms before the first of the year, "forever free" would be off the table. Lincoln wouldn't strike at slavery in the CSA.

We on the side of black liberty, like those opposed to it, had up to one hundred days to wait.

LEFT Detail of *The Aftermath at Bloody Lane* (1889), oil on canvas by James Hope. "Bloody Lane" was a sunken road, eight hundred yards long, where some five thousand Union and Confederate soldiers lay dead and wounded by 1:00 p.m. on September 17, during the Battle of Antietam, also known as the Battle of Sharpsburg. All told, there were more than twenty thousand casualties. The artist was a captain in the Second Vermont Infantry. Because of illness, he didn't see action, but he was well enough to sketch battle scenes, which he later turned into panoramic paintings (twelve feet wide) like this one.

ABOVE Abraham Lincoln, Preliminary Proclamation, September 1862. This is page two of the now four-page decree.

Writing the Emancipation Proclamation (ca. 1864), by Adalbert Johann Volck, a Confederate sympathizer. In Volck's etching, Lincoln looks sinister as he scribbles on a table with legs that taper into cloven hooves (associated with the devil in some cultures). Instead of respecting the Constitution, Lincoln uses it as a footrest. Also adding to the sense of menace: the little demon holding the inkwell, the bats or vultures outside the window, the curtain's vulture-head tieback.

In the corner is the personification of America, Lady Columbia, with a cap over her face. This is an allusion to Lincoln's secret entry into Washington, D.C., right before his inauguration because of an alleged plot to kill him in Baltimore. It was rumored that part of his disguise was a Scottish cap.

The small drawing on the back wall, "St. Ossawatomie," implies that Lincoln idolized John Brown. (In 1856, several months after the Pottawatomie massacre, John Brown lost a son and several other comrades in a battle with proslavery activists in Osawatomie, Kansas.)

The larger drawing, "St. Domingo," alludes to the way blacks in Haiti achieved their independence from France: through violence, just as white colonists in America had gained theirs from England. But Volck was not focused on that similarity but rather on fueling fear of black people.

The decanter and glasses on the small table suggest that the president was drinking as he penned the Emancipation Proclamation.

Abraham Lincoln Writing the Emancipation Proclamation (1863), oil on canvas by David Gilmour Blythe, a Union loyalist. The artist imagined Lincoln working on the Emancipation Proclamation disheveled and in his stocking feet. The messy room is full of symbolism and history. For starters, the window curtain is an upside-down American flag—not a sign of disrespect but a signal of distress.

To the president's right is a pile of petitions, books (one on the Constitution), and other documents (one from the border states). On Lincoln's lap is a copy of the Constitution and the Bible. The couch is covered with petitions for emancipation and protests (including one about soldiers having to be bothered with "contrabands").

At Lincoln's feet are maps. The one of the Confederate states is held down by a rail-splitter's maul—a sledgehammer—used in making fence rails. (At one point, Lincoln was a rail-splitter, and during the 1860 presidential campaign some of his boosters seized upon the idea of promoting him as "the Rail Splitter," to increase his appeal to working-class voters.)

Two items hold down the map of South Carolina: a bundle of rods (*fasci*, Latin), a symbol of power and authority from ancient Rome, and a ball of Greek fire (an ancient fire bomb).

Watch Meeting—Dec. 31st 1862—Waiting for the Hour (1863), oil on canvas by William Tolman Carlton. It's five minutes from midnight, and most eyes are on the elderly man's pocket watch, its fob in the shape of an anchor, a symbol of hope for Christians. Torchlit and nailed to the wall hangs a copy of the Emancipation Proclamation.

PART III

"THE TRUMP OF JUBILEE"

"WE WERE WAITING AND LISTENING AS FOR A BOLT FROM the sky, . . . we were watching, as it were, by the dim light of the stars, for the dawn of a new day; we were longing for the answer to the agonizing prayers of centuries." So remembered Frederick Douglass.

Eight o'clock.

Nine o'clock.

Ten o'clock.

Hour by hour, Douglass, Anna E. Dickinson, J. Sella Martin, and the rest of the crowd at Tremont Temple clung to hope, while braced for a blow.

We had never taken anything for granted.

> *Respectfully solicits a brief interview on the subject of <u>Colonizing</u> the Island of A'Vache, (Hayti), with Contrabands.*
>
> *If not convenient This morning, will the President please indicate when he will grant, an audience.*

Bernard Kock to Abraham Lincoln, Saturday, October 4, 1862. This note accompanied the calling card of developer Bernard Kock, so-called governor of Île à Vache (Cow Island), off the coast of Haiti. Kock convinced Lincoln that Île à Vache was an ideal place to colonize blacks from America. Chiriquí no longer looked so good. For starters, the Chiriquí Improvement Company's claim of land ownership proved suspect and reports of high-quality coal on the land false. On New Year's Eve 1862, while many were praying for the Emancipation Proclamation, Lincoln contracted with Kock to relocate five thousand blacks to Île à Vache for fifty dollars per person. In the end, only 450 people went.

During the hundred days' wait, we had heard reports of Union soldiers grumbling about Lincoln's emancipation decree: sucking their teeth over the prospect of fighting not only for the Union but also for black liberty.

We had also witnessed Republican defeats in the midterm elections. Losses included more than thirty seats in the House of Representatives and the governorship of New York. There, the winner, Horatio Seymour, had roundly condemned the Emancipation Proclamation.

And there was a puzzling, troubling proposal in Lincoln's December 1862 Annual Message to Congress. The president advocated amending the Constitution to (1) make "forever free" enslaved people who had experienced "actual freedom" during the war (with compensation to their owners, provided they were Union loyalists); (2) empower Congress to fund "and otherwise provide" for black emigration anywhere outside America; and (3) compensate *any* state that agreed to abolish slavery by January 1. But not in 1863.

In 1900.

If what he proposed became constitutional law, the war would end "now" and the Union would be saved "forever," Lincoln argued. And he closed on a soaring note, what many historians regard as his greatest peroration, that is the end of a speech:

> Fellow-citizens, *we* cannot escape history. We of this Congress and this administration, will be remembered in spite of ourselves. . . . The fiery trial through which we pass, will light us down, in honor or dishonor, to the latest generation. . . . We know how to save the Union. . . . In *giving* freedom to the *slave*, we *assure* freedom to the *free*—honorable alike in what we give, and what we preserve. We shall nobly save, or meanly lose, the last best, hope of earth. Other means may succeed; this could not fail. The way is plain, peaceful, generous, just—a way which, if followed, the world will forever applaud, and God must forever bless.

What Lincoln recommended was not to be a substitute for the Emancipation Proclamation. Still, Congress did not oblige him.

On the night of January 1, 1863, at Tremont Temple, pocket watches were moving on eleven o'clock when word spread that Lincoln had signed the proclamation of liberation.

One very impatient member of the crowd, Judge Thomas Russell, dashed to the offices of the *Boston Journal* to see if the decree had indeed come across that newspaper's wires. Finding that it had, and against the protest of the night editor, the judge snatched the dispatch, then bolted. When he reached Tremont Temple with proof of the proclamation, people whooped and hollered, shouted and sobbed. Bowlers and bonnets confettied the air. Frederick Douglass soon led the crowd in John Brown's favorite hymn, "Blow Ye the Trumpet, Blow."

Earlier, when word that the proclamation was coming across the wires reached Boston's Music Hall, "shouts arose, hats and handkerchiefs were waved, men and women sprang to their feet," reported *The Liberator*. This crowd also hip-hip-hoorayed William Lloyd Garrison.

I BREAK YOUR *bonds and masterships,*

And I unchain the slave:

Free be his heart and hand henceforth,

As wind and wandering wave.

—from Ralph Waldo Emerson's poem "Boston Hymn," which he read early on during the wait at the Music Hall

Like Emerson, Garrison would join Wendell Phillips and others at George and Mary Stearns's home in Medford for a John Brown party. The highlight was the special showing of a marble bust of their martyred hero. Another delight was Emerson reciting his "Boston Hymn" and Julia Ward Howe her poem "The Battle Hymn of the Republic," by then a beloved Union marching song.

DOWN IN THE NATION'S CAPITAL, Henry McNeal Turner, pastor of Israel Bethel church, had been in the throng at the *Evening Star*, waiting for a hot-off-the-press copy of that newspaper with the proclamation. Once Turner got hold of a copy, he tore down Pennsylvania Avenue. "I ran as for my life, and when the people saw me coming with the paper in my hand they raised a shouting cheer that was almost deafening."

Back in his pulpit, Turner was so breathless that he ended up handing to another the honor of reading the Emancipation Proclamation aloud.

It said nothing about *gradual* liberation.

Nothing about compensation for a single slaveholder.

Nothing about forcing—or even urging—blacks to emigrate.

What's more, Lincoln had signed off on black men serving as soldiers in the Union Army.

During the wait, Lincoln had done quite a bit of revising.

OPPOSITE Boston-born poet, essayist, and philosopher Ralph Waldo Emerson, ca. 1860.

ABOVE Henry McNeal Turner, pastor of D.C.'s first African Methodist Episcopal church. Turner, a native of South Carolina, had never known slavery. This engraving appeared in the December 12, 1863, issue of *Harper's Weekly*. It accompanied an article on Turner's commission as the first black chaplain in the U.S. armed forces.

BY THE PRESIDENT OF THE UNITED STATES OF AMERICA

A PROCLAMATION

Whereas on the 22d day of September, A.D. 1862, a proclamation was issued by the President of the United States, containing, among other things, the following, to wit:

Below, Lincoln quotes parts of the preliminary proclamation.

"That on the 1st day of January, A.D. 1863, all persons held as slaves within any State or designated part of a State the people whereof shall then be in rebellion against the United States shall be then, thenceforward, and forever free; and the executive government of the United States, including the military and naval authority thereof, will recognize and maintain the freedom of such persons and will do no act or acts to repress such persons, or any of them, in any efforts they may make for their actual freedom.

"That the executive will on the 1st day of January aforesaid, by proclamation, designate the States and parts of States, if any, in which the people thereof, respectively, shall then be in rebellion against the United States; and the fact that any State or the people thereof shall on that day be in good faith represented in the Congress of the United States by members chosen thereto at elections wherein a majority of the qualified voters of such States shall have participated shall, in the absence of strong countervailing testimony, be deemed conclusive evidence that such State and the people thereof are not then in rebellion against the United States."

Lincoln now proceeds with his final proclamation.

Now, therefore, I, Abraham Lincoln, President of the United States, by virtue of the power in me vested as Commander in Chief of the Army and Navy of the United States in time of actual armed rebellion against the authority and Government of the United States, and as a fit and necessary war measure for suppressing said rebellion, do, on this 1st day of January, A.D. 1863, and in accordance with my purpose so to do, publicly proclaimed for the full period of one hundred days from the day first above mentioned, order and designate as the States and parts of States wherein the people thereof, respectively, are this day in rebellion against the United States the following, to wit:

Arkansas, Texas, Louisiana (except the parishes of St. Bernard, Plaquemines, Jefferson, St. John, St. Charles, St. James, Ascension, Assumption, Terrebonne, Lafourche, St. Mary, St. Martin, and Orleans, including the city of New Orleans), Mississippi, Alabama, Florida, Georgia, South Carolina, North Carolina, and Virginia (except the forty-eight counties designated as West Virginia, and also the counties of Berkeley, Accomac, Northampton, Elizabeth City, York, Princess Anne, and Norfolk, including the cities of

Norfolk and Portsmouth), and which excepted parts are for the present left precisely as if this proclamation were not issued.

The paragraph above states where the Proclamation applies: All eight states that are still in rebellion: Alabama, Arkansas, Florida, Georgia, Mississippi, North Carolina, South Carolina, and Texas. Certain parts of Louisiana and Virginia are exempted because they are under Union occupation and so technically no longer in rebellion. The Proclamation does not apply to Tennessee for the same reason. However, Lincoln does not exempt some other Union-occupied places, most notably the South Carolina sea islands, where black troops were recruited and where about ten thousand blacks live. Given the Union troop presence in the area, the Proclamation can be enforced there, and so freedom is immediate. Another estimated forty thousand people are also actually freed because they, too, are in Union-occupied territory where the Proclamation applies.

Of the roughly four million people enslaved, the Proclamation doesn't apply to about eight hundred thousand (about five hundred thousand of whom are in the border states).

And by virtue of the power and for the purpose aforesaid, I do order and declare that all persons held as slaves within said designated States and parts of States are, and henceforward shall be free, and that the executive government of the United States, including the military and naval authorities thereof, will recognize and maintain the freedom of said persons.

Unlike earlier versions, the Proclamation does not declare anyone free "forever." This no doubt reflects Lincoln's acute awareness that his war measure didn't guarantee anything and that there was no telling what might happen after the war.

And I hereby enjoin upon the people so declared to be free to abstain from all violence, unless in necessary self-defense; and I recommend to them that in all cases when allowed they labor faithfully for reasonable wages.

Blacks are urged to not riot and to not shrink from work for fair pay.

And I further declare and make known that such persons of suitable condition will be received into the armed service of the United States to garrison forts, positions, stations, and other places and to man vessels of all sorts in said service.

Blacks can be soldiers in the Union Army.

And upon this act, sincerely believed to be an act of justice, warranted by the Constitution upon military necessity, I invoke the considerate judgment of mankind and the gracious favor of Almighty God.

This reiterates the *official* reason for the proclamation—"military necessity"—followed by some noble sentiments. Treasury Secretary Chase had suggested this when Lincoln met with his cabinet to review the document one last time. Earlier, Charles Sumner had told Lincoln that the proclamation had to say something about "'justice' & 'God.'"

In witness whereof I have hereunto set my hand and caused the seal of the United States to be affixed.

Done at the city of Washington, this 1st day of January, A.D. 1863, and of the Independence of the United States of America the eighty-seventh.

Abraham Lincoln

By the President:

William H. Seward
Secretary of State

Emancipation Day in South Carolina from the January 24, 1863, issue of *Frank Leslie's Illustrated Newspaper*.

Festivities were under way earlier in the day, in Port Royal, South Carolina, home of the First South Carolina Volunteers: the first fruits of the order on raising black troops that Secretary of War Stanton had given General Saxton months earlier.

On New Year's Eve 1862, Lincoln had alerted Saxton and other top military men that he would be signing the Emancipation Proclamation. So, on New Year's Day 1863, while most of the nation was still waiting, the Port Royal celebration started, around noon, in a grove of live oaks.

After prayer, there was a reading aloud of a near-final draft of the proclamation by William Henry Brisbane, a slaveholder turned abolitionist some thirty years earlier.

The Port Royal program didn't go exactly as planned. At one point, blacks went off-script.

It started with one man. "There suddenly arose, close beside the platform, a strong male voice (but rather cracked and elderly)," remembered Colonel Thomas Wentworth Higginson. And, in a flash, two black women joined in. The three were singing a patriotic hymn:

Thomas Wentworth Higginson, commander of the First South Carolina Volunteers. This Massachusetts native was a member of the John Brown Secret Six.

> *My country, 'tis of thee*
> *Sweet land of liberty*
> *Of thee I sing . . .*

"People looked at each other," wrote Higginson, "and then at us on the platform, to see whence came this interruption."

No matter the dismay of those on the dais, the singers didn't waver, didn't flinch. "Firmly and irrepressibly, the quavering voices sang on, verse after verse." Soon, other blacks were singing, too. And if Harriet Tubman was on the scene, as is believed, surely she gave her all to the song.

As whites also began to sing, Higginson signaled them to hush—to just listen. "I never saw anything so electric; it made all other words cheap; it seemed the choked voice of a race at last unloosed."

Charlotte Forten (ca. 1870), a member of one of Philadelphia's most prominent black families. (Her wealthy grandfather, James Forten, had given William Lloyd Garrison moral and financial support during *The Liberator*'s early days.) In the fall of 1862, Charlotte Forten headed south to teach "contrabands" on St. Helena, South Carolina, and thus to take part in the Port Royal Experiment. In this program, started earlier in the year after the Union capture of Port Royal Island, Northern reformers committed money and supplies—and, for some, their teaching skills—to aid blacks whose owners had fled Port Royal and other sea islands. The goal of the Port Royal Experiment was twofold: to help these people build new lives and to prove to white skeptics that freed blacks could be absorbed into society.

THE MOST GLORIOUS *day this nation has yet seen, I think . . . I cannot give a regular chronicle of the day. It is impossible. I was in such a state of excitement. It all seemed, and seems still, like a brilliant dream. . . . As I sat on the stand and looked around on the various groups, I thought I had never seen a sight so beautiful. There were the black soldiers . . . and crowds of lookers-on, men, women and children, grouped in various attitudes, under the trees. The faces of all wore a happy, eager, expectant look.*

—Charlotte Forten in her diary, remembering the Port Royal celebration

W. G. Jackman's engraving of Sandy Cornish from *After the War: A Southern Tour* (1866), by Whitelaw Reid.

Festivals of freedom abounded in the days to come: in Chicago, Illinois; in Columbus, Ohio; in Philadelphia, Pennsylvania, and in Pittsburgh, too. There were even celebrations where the Emancipation Proclamation *did not* apply—in Norfolk, Virginia, for example, which was exempt because it was already under Union control. There, according to a *New York Times* reporter based at Fort Monroe, some four thousand blacks "paraded through the principal streets" behind a fife and drum band.

About a thousand miles south, in Union-occupied Key West, Florida, a similar parade was headed by Sandy Cornish, who some twenty years earlier had hacked at his own body to avoid being re-enslaved.

At jubilee after jubilee, President Lincoln was lionized. People sang his praises.

Why? Some then and many in the future would frown. Why did blacks, especially, lift up Lincoln's name? Hadn't he lobbied for them to leave the nation? Didn't the Emancipation Proclamation declare blacks free where the U.S. government had no actual power but left so many enslaved where it did—most notably in the border states?

All true.

But as Frederick Douglass wrote of that long day's wait, "It was not logic, but the trump of jubilee, which everybody wanted to hear."

We weren't stupid. Like Lincoln, we knew the proclamation was a *war* measure and not an ironclad law. So we knew that the fight for absolute abolition still had to be waged. But on Thursday, January 1, 1863, so many who believed in freedom looked beyond the proclamation's "whereas" and "whereof," the geographic particulars, the tenses and technicalities.

In a leap of faith, we claimed this decree as the dawn of a new day, as an amen!—a thunderbolt "So be it!"—to all those "agonizing prayers of centuries."

IT SHALL FLASH *through coming ages;*
It shall light the distant years;
And eyes now dim with sorrow
Shall be clearer through their tears.

—from Frances E. W. Harper's "President Lincoln's Proclamation of Freedom"
(ca. 1863)

Freed Negroes Spreading the News of President Lincoln's Emancipation Proclamation (Les Negres Affranchis colportant le decret d'affranchisement du President Lincoln), from the March 21, 1863, issue of the French newspaper *Le Monde Illustré*. The scene depicted occurred near Winchester, Virginia.

EPILOGUE

SLAVERY HAS EXISTED *in this country too long and has stamped its character too deeply and indelibly, to be blotted out in a day or a year, or even in a generation. The slave will yet remain in some sense a slave, long after the chains are taken from his limbs, and the master will yet retain much of the pride, the arrogance, imperiousness and conscious superiority, and love of power, acquired by his former relation of master. Time, necessity, education, will be required to bring all classes into harmonious and natural relations. . . .*

Law and the sword can and will, in the end abolish slavery. But law and the sword cannot abolish the malignant slaveholding sentiment which has kept the slave system alive in this country during two centuries. Pride of race, prejudice against color, will raise this hateful clamor for oppression of the negro as heretofore. The slave having ceased to be the abject slave of a single master, his enemies will endeavor to make him the slave of society at large.

—Frederick Douglass at Spring Street AME Zion Church in Rochester, New York,
on December 28, 1862

Minds mightier than mine have debated and will continue to debate the answer to the question "Who freed the slaves?"

Lincoln? The abolitionists? The Republican-dominated Congress? The Union Army? The stiff-necked border states (by not saying yes to compensated, gradual compensation)? The slaveholding Southern aristocracy (the force behind secession)? The enslaved people themselves? God? Or, as historian Lerone Bennett Jr. has pondered, was it History?

And there's that other great debate: Was Lincoln wrapped tight in racism, or was he shedding that skin as the war ensued? Or was he really not a racist at all, but simply "a man of his times"? While I can appreciate the debate intellectually, I'm not consumed by it.

Nor do I fume over the fact that the Emancipation Proclamation is a dull document that makes our eyes glaze over, possessing "all the moral grandeur of a bill of lading," as the historian Richard Hofstadter famously put it. Considering that it is a military order, I can't fault it for being devoid of passionate prose.

And if truth be told, I don't care if Lincoln issued the Emancipation Proclamation as a military necessity, as a moral necessity, or because he had a dream. For me, what matters is that people in bondage—folk from whom I descend— were at long last freed. Lincoln's Emancipation Proclamation was a milestone in the march to final freedom. It changed so much.

The Emancipation Proclamation emboldened more enslaved children and adults—one by one, two by two, in groups—to walk, run, sail, swim to Union lines, claiming freedom and creating a labor drain and more chaos in the Confederacy.

The Emancipation Proclamation fired up nearly 200,000 black men—134,000 from the CSA and the border states—to join the Union armed forces, ready to prove themselves battle-brave, and well aware that if the Confederacy won, final freedom might be a far-off thing.

As well, the Emancipation Proclamation spoke to the "better angels" of many white men in the Union—men more willing than some first imagined to give life and limb for both preservation of the Union *and* black liberty. It prompted more than a few whites not heretofore in Union blue to go marching off to war—a war the Union won.

Finally, the Emancipation Proclamation was the prologue for the actual Thirteenth Amendment: not the one a panicked, scrambling Congress, hoping to prevent a civil war, passed back in March 1861— the one that would have banned the legislative branch from ever abolishing slavery in the states, the amendment that never went anywhere because only two states ratified it (Maryland and Ohio, with Illinois endorsing it during a constitutional convention). No, not that original Thirteenth Amendment but the one that came four years later, ending chattel slavery in America—an amendment Lincoln vigorously supported.

Given all this, I can't help but honor Lincoln's Emancipation Proclamation—can't help but respect what it meant to all those who waited so long for that trump of jubilee, that dawn of liberty: souls who knew about those agonizing prayers of centuries in a way that I never will.

PREVIOUS SPREAD *Lee Surrendering to Grant at Appomattox* (ca. 1870), oil on paperboard by Alonzo Chappel. When the CSA's top general, Robert E. Lee, surrendered to the Union's top general, Ulysses S. Grant, on April 9, 1865, in Appomattox, Virginia, the Civil War was essentially over.

OPPOSITE Harriet Tubman in her early nineties (ca. 1912), roughly fifty years after the Emancipation Proclamation was issued. This photograph was taken outside her home in Auburn, New York.

THE THIRTEENTH AMENDMENT

This amendment passed in Congress on January 31, 1865. It was ratified by the necessary three-fourths of the states on December 6, 1865.

SECTION 1.

Neither slavery nor involuntary servitude, except as a punishment for crime whereof the party shall have been duly convicted, shall exist within the United States, or any place subject to their jurisdiction.

SECTION 2.

Congress shall have power to enforce this article by appropriate legislation.

Fifty-five-year-old Abraham Lincoln on February 5, 1865, photographed by Alexander Gardner. Weeks later, on April 11, the president gave a speech from a White House balcony on the nation's reunion, now that the war was over. Lincoln expressed support for some black men—"the very intelligent" and "those who serve our cause as soldiers"—having the right to vote. "That is the last speech he will ever make," one member of the crowd reportedly said. It was John Wilkes Booth, a Confederate sympathizer from the border state of Maryland. Three days later, on Good Friday, Booth fatally shot the president.

TIMELINE

This Civil War timeline is not comprehensive but rather offers some of the key events.
Space does not permit inclusion of all the major military battles.

1860

FEBRUARY 27 Lincoln rails against slavery in the territories at New York City's Cooper Institute.

APRIL 23—MAY 3 At a convention in Charleston, South Carolina, the Democratic Party splits over slavery in the territories. One faction (mostly Northerners) insists that it should be a matter of popular sovereignty. The other faction (mostly Southerners) wants the party to stand for a guarantee that slaveholders can move into the territories with their human property.

MAY 16—18 At its convention in Chicago, the Republican Party chooses Lincoln as its presidential candidate and Senator Hannibal Hamlin of Maine as his running mate.

JUNE 18—23 At a convention in Baltimore, "Popular Sovereignty" Democrats pick Lincoln's old rival, Illinois Senator Stephen Douglas, as their presidential candidate and Herschel Vespasian Johnson, former governor of Georgia, as his running mate.

JUNE 28 At a convention in Richmond, Virginia, the faction of largely Southern Democrats picks the sitting vice president, John Cabell Breckinridge of Kentucky, as the party's presidential candidate and Senator Joseph Lane of Oregon as his running mate.

NOVEMBER 6 The Lincoln-Hamlin ticket wins the presidential election.

DECEMBER 3 A proslavery mob attacks Frederick Douglass, William Lloyd Garrison, and other abolitionists in Boston's Tremont Temple. This happens during a commemoration of John Brown.

DECEMBER 20 South Carolina secedes.

1861

JANUARY 9—26 Mississippi, Florida, Alabama, Georgia, and then Louisiana secede.

JANUARY 29 Kansas joins the U.S. as a free state.

FEBRUARY 1 Texas issues its Ordinance of Secession.

FEBRUARY 4—9 The CSA is formed with Jefferson Davis as president during a convention in Montgomery, Alabama, the Confederacy's first capital.

MARCH 2 Congress approves a thirteenth amendment that would prevent Congress from abolishing slavery in any state where it exists. This amendment will go nowhere because only two state legislatures ratify it: Ohio in May 1861, and Maryland in January 1862. It was also in 1862 that Illinois approved the amendment, but it did so at a constitutional convention and therefore on legally shaky ground.

MARCH 4 Lincoln is inaugurated the sixteenth U.S. president. In his address, he pushes for peace.

APRIL 12—14 Fort Sumter is attacked, surrenders to CSA forces, and is evacuated.

APRIL 15 Lincoln issues a proclamation calling state militias to send a total of 75,000 troops to suppress the rebellion. He also orders Congress to return to work on July 4.

APRIL 17 Virginia issues its Ordinance of Secession.

APRIL 19 A pro-CSA mob attacks U.S. troops in Baltimore. *Also on this day:* Lincoln issues a proclamation for a naval blockade of ports in South Carolina, Georgia, Alabama, Florida, Mississippi, Louisiana, and Texas.

APRIL 27 Lincoln extends the naval blockade to include Virginia and North Carolina. Though North Carolina hasn't yet seceded, its officials are seizing federal property (just as in the states that have seceded), refusing to hand over revenue due, and in other ways engaging in rebellion. *Also on this day:* Lincoln suspends the writ of habeas corpus along troop routes between Philadelphia and Washington, D.C., thus allowing the army to jail subversives without charges. (In September 1862, Lincoln will suspend the writ of habeas corpus throughout America.)

MAY 6 Arkansas secedes.

MAY 13 Baltimore is put under martial law.

MAY 20 North Carolina secedes. *Also on this day:* Kentucky proclaims neutrality.

MAY 24 U.S. General Benjamin Butler defies the Fugitive Slave Law at Fort Monroe.

MAY 29 Jefferson Davis arrives in Richmond, Virginia, as the CSA capital moves there from Montgomery, Alabama.

JUNE 8 Tennessee secedes.

JUNE 11—25 Representatives from western counties in Virginia meet in Wheeling to officially repudiate Virginia's secession. They declare themselves the "Restored Government of Virginia."

JULY 21 First Battle of Bull Run/Manassas (Virginia): The CSA victory disabuses people in the North of the notion that suppressing the rebellion will be a cakewalk.

AUGUST 6 U.S. Congress passes and Lincoln signs into law the first Confiscation Act.

AUGUST 30 U.S. General John C. Frémont, chief of the Union Army's Western Department, puts Missouri under martial law and declares free those people held in slavery by supporters of the rebellion.

SEPTEMBER 11 Lincoln rescinds Frémont's freedom decree.

DECEMBER 3 In his Annual Message to Congress, Lincoln proposes colonizing blacks.

DECEMBER 16 Inaugural meeting of the Emancipation League, cofounded by Wendell Phillips.

1862

JANUARY 10 The *New York Times* reports: "The President shall acquire in Mexico, South America, Central America, or islands in the Gulf of Mexico, lands, or the right of settlement on lands, to which emancipated slaves shall be transported, single persons receiving forty acres of land, and married persons eighty acres."

MARCH 6 Lincoln asks the U.S. Congress to support compensated, gradual emancipation.

MARCH 13 U.S. Congress passes and Lincoln signs into law an additional article of war, banning military officers from returning people who escaped slavery to their owners.

APRIL 10 U.S. Congress signs off on compensated, gradual emancipation.

APRIL 11 U.S. Congress passes the D.C. Emancipation Act, which includes compensation for slaveholders and $100,000 for colonizing blacks.

APRIL 16 Slavery is abolished in Washington, D.C., when Lincoln signs the Emancipation Act into law. Scholars debate why he waited five days.

MAY 9 U.S. General David Hunter, commander of the Department of the South, declares South Carolina, Georgia, and Florida under martial law and the people enslaved in those states free.

MAY 13 Robert Smalls, with family members and friends, escapes slavery in South Carolina aboard the CSA vessel *Planter*. He will become captain of the boat as a member of the Union Navy.

MAY 19 Lincoln revokes General Hunter's freedom decree of May 9.

JUNE 19 U.S. Congress passes and Lincoln signs into law the bill prohibiting slavery in U.S. Territories.

JULY 12 Lincoln meets with representatives of the border states on compensated, gradual emancipation.

JULY 14 The majority of representatives from the border states reject compensated, gradual emancipation.

JULY 17 U.S. Congress passes and Lincoln signs into law the second Confiscation and the Militia Acts.

JULY 22 Lincoln discusses the Emancipation Proclamation with his cabinet.

SUMMER J. Sella Martin buys his sister and her daughter and son out of slavery in Columbus, Georgia, for about $2,000. He raised the money while lecturing in England.

CIRCA AUGUST The Contraband Relief Association is founded to provide material support and other help to blacks flooding into Washington, D.C., in their escapes from slavery. The organization is spearheaded by Elizabeth Keckley, dressmaker of the Union's First Lady, Mary Todd Lincoln. Keckley had purchased her and her son's freedom in the 1850s (in Missouri).

AUGUST 14 At the White House, Lincoln talks to a black delegation about colonization.

AUGUST 20 Horace Greeley publishes his letter to Lincoln, "The Prayer of Twenty Millions," in his newspaper, the *New-York Tribune*, taking him to task for not moving boldly against slavery.

AUGUST 23 Lincoln's response to Greeley is published. Its most famous passage: "My paramount object in this struggle *is* to save the Union, and *is not* either to save or to destroy slavery."

AUGUST 25 Secretary of War Stanton authorizes General Rufus Saxton in South Carolina to raise black troops.

SEPTEMBER 17 Battle of Antietam/ Sharpsburg (Maryland): Union forces under the command of General George B. McClellan stop the invasion of Union soil by CSA forces under the command of General Robert E. Lee.

SEPTEMBER 22 Lincoln issues the preliminary Emancipation Proclamation.

OCTOBER 22 Charlotte Forten sails from a New York port to South Carolina, where she will teach "contrabands" on St. Helena.

DECEMBER 1 In his Annual Message to Congress, Lincoln advocates compensation to Union loyalists for the loss of enslaved people; compensated, gradual emancipation; and colonization.

DECEMBER 31 Lincoln contracts with Bernard Kock to transport blacks to Île à Vache, off Haiti's southwestern peninsula.

1863

JANUARY 1 Lincoln issues the final **EMANCIPATION PROCLAMATION**.

JANUARY 12 In a message to his Congress, CSA President Jefferson Davis declares the Emancipation Proclamation an abomination that makes reunion "forever impossible."

FEBRUARY 24 Frederick Douglass becomes a recruiter for black regiments. (Two of his sons, Charles and Lewis, will serve in one: the Fifty-fourth Massachusetts Infantry.)

APRIL 14 About 450 blacks sail from Fort Monroe aboard the *Ocean Ranger* to start a colony on Île à Vache, Haiti.

MAY 1 The CSA Congress authorizes the execution or enslavement of captured black soldiers. The CSA has already declared white officers of black troops worthy of death.

MAY 6 Abolitionists gather at Boston's Tremont Temple to celebrate and hear an address from Thomas Simms. A few weeks earlier, in Mississippi, this black man (along with his family and friends) made it to Union troops under the command of General Ulysses S. Grant (about to start the siege of Vicksburg). After Simms and company gave Grant's forces intelligence on the Confederates, they headed for Boston with a safe-passage certificate from Grant. Back in 1851, Sims was arrested in Boston for escaping slavery. His return to the South and to slavery was something Wendell Phillips and other abolitionists tried to stop.

JUNE 2 With Union Colonel James Montgomery, Harriet Tubman leads about three hundred black troops in a raid along the Combahee River (near Beaufort, South Carolina). It results in the destruction of a CSA supply depot and other property and the liberation of about seven hundred blacks.

JUNE 20 West Virginia enters the Union with a gradual emancipation plan in place, a condition Lincoln and Congress had imposed.

AUGUST 10 Frederick Douglass meets with Lincoln to demand equal pay for black troops. White privates received $13 a month plus a clothing allowance of $3.50. Black troops, no matter rank, received $10 a month, with $3 *deducted* from their pay for clothing.

OCTOBER 17 The *New York Times* reports on blacks who left America to start a colony on Île à Vache, Haiti: "Information has reached here that these colonists were badly provided for, and many of them died from disease, while others fled to more desirable localities."

NOVEMBER 6 Henry McNeal Turner becomes the first black chaplain in the Union Army, by Lincoln appointment. (Turner will serve with a black regiment for which his church has been a recruiting center.)

NOVEMBER 19 In the ceremony dedicating the Gettysburg battlefield a national cemetery, Lincoln delivers his shortest and most famous speech, the Gettysburg Address. It begins: "Fourscore and seven years ago our fathers brought forth on this continent a new nation, conceived in liberty and dedicated to the proposition that all men are created equal." It ends with the hope that America "shall have a new birth of freedom, and that government of the people, by the people, for the people shall not perish from the earth." The Battle of Gettysburg (July 1–3, 1863), which put a stop to the CSA invasion of Northern soil, was the bloodiest battle of the war. Of the combined 158,000 Union and Confederate forces, there were some 51,000 casualties.

DECEMBER 2 The Capitol's dome is completed with the installation of the last sections of its crowning glory: the bronze Statue of Freedom.

DECEMBER 8 Lincoln issues Proclamation of Amnesty and Reconstruction. It offers full pardon and return of property (except people) to most Confederates if they pledge allegiance to the Union and accept emancipation. It also outlines the process for the Confederate states to be restored to the Union. Most important requirement: a new state constitution that abolishes slavery. By now, the Union is in control of many CSA major ports and capital cities.

1864

JANUARY 16 Twenty-one-year-old Anna E. Dickinson makes history as the first woman to give a speech to the U.S. Congress.

Her topic: "The Perils of the Hour." She takes Lincoln to task for his moderation but in the end expresses her support of him. Lincoln and the First Lady are in attendance for part of the speech. (In the fall of 1863, Dickinson stumped for Republican candidates. In the fall of 1864, she will do so again.)

FEBRUARY 1 Lincoln directs Secretary of War Stanton to send a ship to Île à Vache to bring back the black colonists who wish to return.

MARCH 16 In its new state constitution Union-held Arkansas abolishes slavery.

MARCH 20 A little over 350 of the roughly 450 blacks who emigrated to Île à Vache return to the U.S. aboard the Marcia C. Day.

APRIL 8 A new thirteenth amendment to the Constitution, one to abolish chattel slavery in America, passes in the U.S. Senate (38–6).

JUNE 7–8 In a convention in Baltimore, Lincoln is nominated for a second term by the Republican Party (temporarily calling itself the National Union Party).

JUNE 15 U.S. Congress passes a bill mandating that black soldiers receive the same pay as white soldiers.

JUNE 28 U.S. Congress repeals the Fugitive Slave Law.

JULY 1 (APPROXIMATELY) Garrison sends to Lincoln William Tolman Carlton's painting Watch Meeting—Dec. 31st 1862—Waiting for the Hour. It was purchased by a group of Boston women and given to the president at Garrison's urging.

JULY 2 U.S. Congress passes a bill eliminating any further funding for colonization.

SEPTEMBER 2 Fall of Atlanta: U.S. forces under command of General William Tecumseh Sherman occupy the CSA's munitions "capital."

SEPTEMBER 5 In its new state constitution Union-held Louisiana abolishes slavery.

NOVEMBER 1 Slavery is abolished in Maryland in a new state constitution approved in September.

NOVEMBER 8 Lincoln wins reelection, beating the Democratic Party candidate General George B. McClellan, a former general-in-chief of the Union Army. Lincoln's vice president is the Tennessee Democrat Andrew Johnson, whom the president had made military governor of Tennessee back in 1862.

NOVEMBER 15 Leaving Atlanta in ruins, and with a 62,000-man army, Union general William Tecumseh Sherman begins a campaign of destruction en route to coastal Georgia: his "March to the Sea."

NOVEMBER 28 Frances E. W. Harper attends a celebration (at New York City's Cooper Institute) of the abolition of slavery in Maryland, where she was born. (She is on her way to Maryland, where she will spend time with Frederick Douglass, who had not set foot in his home state in about twenty years. Harper, recently widowed, will settle in Philadelphia and resume writing and lecturing for social justice.)

DECEMBER 22 Sherman sends Lincoln a telegram from Georgia: "I beg to present you as a Christmas gift the city of Savannah with 150 heavy guns & plenty of ammunition & also about 25,000 bales of cotton."

1865

JANUARY 11 Missouri abolishes slavery within in its borders.

JANUARY 21 Garrison writes Lincoln, bewildered that the president never acknowledged receipt of the painting *Watch Meeting—Dec. 31st 1862—Waiting for the Hour.* Garrison knows (from Charles Sumner) that the painting is in the White House.

JANUARY 31 U.S. House of Representatives finally approves the Thirteenth Amendment (119–56).

FEBRUARY 1 Lincoln's Illinois is the first state to ratify the Thirteenth Amendment.

FEBRUARY 3 West Virginia abolishes slavery.

FEBRUARY 5 Lincoln shares with his cabinet a plan for ending the war and slavery: offer all slaveholding states $400 million, half if hostilities cease on or before April 1 and half when the Thirteenth Amendment is adopted. (Lincoln calculated that $400 million was about the cost of one hundred days of war.) The cabinet opposes the scheme; the president scraps it.

FEBRUARY 7 Lincoln sends Garrison a note apologizing for his tardy thank-you for *Watch Meeting—Dec. 31st 1862—Waiting for the Hour,* which he calls a "spirited and admirable painting."

FEBRUARY 22 Union-held Tennessee abolishes slavery in an amendment to its constitution.

MARCH 3 Congress passes and Lincoln signs into law a bill creating America's first government-run social welfare agency: the Bureau of Refugees, Freedmen, and Abandoned Lands (known as the Freedmen's Bureau).

MARCH 4 Lincoln delivers his second Inaugural Address. His closing begins: "With malice toward none; with charity for all; with firmness in the right, as God gives us to see the right, let us strive on to finish the work we are in; to bind up the nation's wounds."

MARCH 13 CSA president Jefferson Davis signs into a law a bill that allows blacks to serve in combat.

APRIL 3 Union troops take Richmond, Virginia, the CSA capital.

APRIL 9 The CSA's General Robert E. Lee surrenders to the Union's General Ulysses S. Grant.

APRIL 11 From a White House balcony, Lincoln gives a speech on the nation's political reconstruction in which he expresses support for limited black suffrage.

APRIL 14 While Lincoln and the First Lady watch a play at Washington, D.C.'s, Ford Theatre, John Wilkes Booth shoots the president in the head.

APRIL 15 Lincoln dies. Vice president Andrew Johnson becomes president.

MAY 9—10 Thirty-second Annual Convention of the American Anti-Slavery Society at the Church of the Puritans in New York City. William Lloyd Garrison calls for the organization to be dissolved because its mission—the abolition of slavery—has essentially been accomplished. Anna E. Dickinson, Frederick Douglass, and Wendell Phillips, among others, disagree. For them "mission accomplished" means achieving black civil and political rights. The society continues with Phillips as president.

MAY 22 Following capture in Georgia, CSA president Jefferson Davis begins a two-year imprisonment in Virginia's Fort Monroe.

JUNE 19 Blacks in Galveston, Texas, learn from Union soldiers that the war is over and that they are free. This is the genesis of the celebration Juneteenth.

DECEMBER 6 The Thirteenth Amendment is ratified by the required three-fourths of the states (twenty-seven of thirty-six). On December 18, it officially becomes part of the Constitution.

DECEMBER 29 The last issue of Garrison's *The Liberator* is published.

GLOSSARY

Definitions of words and phrases are given relative to their use in this book.

abolitionist a person who advocates the end (or abolition) of slavery.

Annual Message to Congress today's State of the Union Address.

batteries places on which to mount guns or fortifications.

broadside a sheet of paper on which is printed an ad, a notice, political message, or other information for public consumption.

ca. abbreviation for "circa," derived from the Latin word *circum* meaning "around."

chattel personal property other than real estate and things tied to it like buildings. In chattel slavery, one person completely owns another. Other types of slavery include debt slavery, in which a person is forced to work for no wages until a debt is paid off.

colonization the act or process of establishing a colony within or without a nation's borders.

Compromise of 1850 a series of laws intended to avoid a civil war over slavery that included the abolition of the slave trade (but not slavery) in Washington, D.C., and a Fugitive Slave Law that made it easier for slaveholders to regain their property from free soil. Also, decisions were made about slavery in territory gained as a result of the U.S.-Mexican War (1846–48): California was admitted to the Union as a free state. The rest was organized into Utah and New Mexico Territories, where slavery was to be a matter of popular sovereignty.

Confederacy shorthand for the Confederate States of America.

Confederate a supporter of the Confederate States of America.

confiscate to take or seize.

Congress (U.S.) national legislative, or lawmaking, body, made up of the Senate and the House of Representatives.

contrabands enslaved blacks who were seized by Union soldiers or given refuge with Union soldiers or other authorities.

Cooper Institute a college founded in 1859, in Lower Manhattan, to offer working-class people a free education.

disunion separation.

Dred Scott decision The March 6, 1857, U.S. Supreme Court ruling in which Dred and Harriet Scott were denied their freedom. The decision also declared that (1) blacks were not and never could be U.S. citizens and (2) the U.S. government could not regulate slavery in the territories.

Faneuil Hall Boston's most famous meeting hall.

free soil a state or territory in which slavery is illegal.

free state a state in which slavery is illegal.

freedom papers a document proving that a person had gained his or her liberty. In some places in the South, blacks who had never been enslaved had certificates attesting to this. It sometimes happened that a person who couldn't produce proof of his or her freedom was sold into slavery.

gradual emancipation freedom rolled out over time or at a set future date.

gutta-percha a hard natural rubber derived from a family of tropical trees that has been used to make golf balls and canes, among other things.

jubilee freedom.

Kansas-Nebraska Act an 1854 law that overturned the ban on slavery in territory above the 36°30' parallel as established by the Missouri Compromise of 1820. Instead, slavery in Kansas and Nebraska was to be a matter of popular sovereignty.

martial law military rule.

Missouri Compromise an 1820 law in which Maine, a former province of Massachusetts, entered the Union as a free state and Missouri as a slave state. As well, slavery was banned in the land acquired in the Louisiana Purchase above the 36°30' parallel (except Missouri).

popular sovereignty doctrine that the people living in a U.S. territory, not the federal government, should be the ones to decide whether to make slavery legal there.

proclamation a statement of a policy to the public at large.

Radical Republican a member of the Republican Party who advocated the immediate abolition of slavery everywhere in America before and during the Civil War and who during Reconstruction pressed for blacks to have civil and political rights. Not until the middle of the twentieth century would changes in the makeup of America's two major political parties lead to a situation in which the Democratic Party was the party more associated with black civil rights.

Rebels (Rebs) what pro-Union people called supporters of the CSA.

rump government a government that has no real authority or power.

secede withdraw.

Secret Six Also known as the Committee of Six, this was a group of men who financed John Brown's antislavery activities in Kansas and his raid on Harpers Ferry. Five of the men were from Massachusetts: physician Samuel Gridley Howe; manufacturer George Stearns; Congregational minister Thomas Wentworth Higginson; Unitarian minister Reverend Theodore Parker; and journalist Frank Sanborn. The sixth man was Gerrit Smith, a millionaire landowner in Peterboro, New York.

servile of or pertaining to someone enslaved.

slave state a state where slavery is legal.

slave trade the bringing of people into the nation or a locality within it for purposes of slavery.

territories lands possessed by the U.S. that are not yet states.

trump the sound of a trumpet; the announcement or proclamation of something joyous in the offing.

Union another name for the United States that grew in popularity during the Civil War.

NOTES

Archaic spellings along with spelling and punctuation errors have been silently corrected.

page vii "Abraham Lincoln was . . .": "Again, Lincoln," *The Crisis*, September 1922, 200.

page vii "A highly secretive . . .": "In Search of the Real Abe Lincoln," *Midwest Today*, February 1993. Posted at http://www.midtod.com/bestof/abe.phtml.

page vii "The problem is . . .": *The Fiery Trial*, xix–xx.

Part I: "The Agonizing Prayers of Centuries"

page 1 "We were waiting . . .": *Life and Times of Frederick Douglass* in *Frederick Douglass: Autobiographies*, 791.

page 2 on Cornish: "From Slavery to Freedom and Success: Sandy Cornish and Lillah Cornish," *Florida Keys Sea Heritage Journal*, Spring 1994, 1, 12–15 and *After the War*, 189–93.

page 8 "I have often . . .": *Narrative of the Life of Frederick Douglass, an American Slave* in *Frederick Douglass: Autobiographies*, 18.

page 8 "I never rise . . .": "Letter from William C. Nell" (quoting Garrison), *The Liberator*, December 14, 1855, 198.

page 9 "The Day of Jubilee": *Songs of the Free*, 199.

page 14 "We do not breathe . . .": "Address to Citizens of Concord," *Emerson's Antislavery Writings*, 53.

page 17 "Hit Him Again": "Embodied Eloquence, the Sumner Assault, and the Transatlantic Cable," *American Literature*, vol 82, no. 3, September 2010, 491.

page 18 "How long will . . .": "Southern Outrages," *The Liberator*, February 22, 1856, 32.

page 21 "We are here . . .": "The Boston Massacre, March 5, 1770," *The Liberator*, March 12, 1858, 43.

page 22 "I know that . . .": "Great Meeting in Boston," *The Liberator*, December 9, 1859, 194.

page 23 "monstrous injustice": "Speech at Peoria, Illinois," *Collected Works of Abraham Lincoln*, vol. 2, 255.

Part II: "A Fit and Necessary Military Measure"

page 25 on Lincoln's racial views: "The Lincoln-Douglas Debates 4th Debate Part I," http://teachingamericanhistory.org/library/index.

asp?document=1048m, "Fifth Debate: Galesburg, Illinois," http://www.nps.gov/liho/historyculture/debate5.htm, and "Lincoln's Black History," http://www.nybooks.com/articles/archives/2009/jun/11/lincolns-black-history/

page 26 "I have no purpose . . .": "First Debate with Stephen A. Douglas at Ottawa, Illinois," *Collected Works of Abraham Lincoln*, vol. 3, 16.

page 26 "Let us have . . .": "Address at Cooper Institute, New York City," *Collected Works of Abraham Lincoln*, vol. 3, 550.

page 28 "the institution of negro . . .": *The Civil War and Reconstruction: A Documentary Collection*, 436.

page 29 "I know what . . .": "Progress," *Speech, Lectures, and Letters*, 384.

pages 28–30 Lincoln's Inaugural Address: "First Inaugural Address—Final Text," *Collected Works of Abraham Lincoln*, vol. 4, 262–71.

page 34 "Are not these Northern people. . .": "Letter from Rev. J. Sella Martin," *Douglass' Monthly*, June 1861, 469.

page 35 "I am credibly . . .": *The Emancipation Proclamation: A Brief History with Documents*, 44.

page 37 on the number of blacks at Fort Monroe: "Imagined Promises, Bitter Realities" in *The Emancipation Proclamation: Three Views*, 1.

page 38 Bull Run data: "Manassas, First," CWSAC Battle Summaries, www.nps.gov/hps/abpp/battles/va005.htm.

pages 38–39 first Confiscation Act: *From Property to Person*, 253–54.

page 39 "alarm our Southern . . .": "To John C. Fremont," *Collected Works of Abraham Lincoln*, vol. 4, 506.

page 40 "I say, *emphatically* . . .": *History of Kentucky*, vol. 1, 87.

page 41 "We cannot conquer . . . use it godlike": *Memoir and Letters of Charles Sumner*, vol. 4, 42.

page 42 "Frémont's proclamation has . . .": "The Hour and the Man," *The Liberator*, September 20, 1861, 150.

page 42 "I think Sumner . . . thunderbolt will keep": *Life and Public Services of Charles Sumner*, 359–60.

page 43 Population data: *The Negro's Civil War*, 321.

pages 43–44 Lincoln's December 1861 Message to Congress: "Annual Message to Congress" *Collected Works of Abraham Lincoln*, vol. 5, 48.

page 45 "an ocean rolling between them," "the elysium of . . ." and "the elysium of . . .": "The Career of a Kansas Politician," *American Historical Review*, vol. 4, October 1898, 101.

page 47 "Slavery is the stomach . . .": "Cast Off the Mill Stone," *Douglass' Monthly*, September 1861, 514.

page 47 Stevens's speech: *The Congressional Globe*, 37th Congress, 2nd Session, 440–41.

page 48 "They may send . . .": *Harriet Tubman*, 298–99.

page 48 Lincoln's March 6, 1862, Message to Congress: "Message to Congress," *Collected Works of Abraham Lincoln*, vol. 5, 144–45.

page 49 "The late message . . .": "Turner on the President's Message," *The Christian Recorder*, March 22, 1862, 46.

page 50–51 on John Harry's petition and payments to slave holders: "Sample of Petition for Owner Compensation" and "List of Owners Who Filed Petitions" "Final Report of the Commission for the Emancipation of Slaves, among DC Emancipation Documents posted os.dc.gov/os/cwp/view,a,1207,q,640006.asp and "End Slavery in the Nation's Capital Booklet" posted at www.os.dc.gov/os/cwp/view,a,1207,q,608954.asp.

page 54 "What I believe is . . .": "Twenty-Ninth Annual Meeting of the American Anti-Slavery Society," *The Liberator*, May 16, 1862, 78.

page 55 "The South, having . . .": "The New England Anti-Slavery Convention," *The Liberator*, June 6, 1862, Transcript at Accessible Archives: www.accessible.com.

page 55 Lincoln's repeal of Hunter's freedom decree: "Proclamation Revoking General Hunter's Order of Military Emancipation of May 9, 1862," *Collected Works of Abraham Lincoln*, vol. 5, 222–23. This document has within it a reprint of Hunter's proclamation.

page 57 "more sacred. . . . You need more . . .": *The Works of Charles Sumner*, vol. 7, 215.

page 57 "Too big a lick": Donald, *Lincoln*, 364.

page 57 Lincoln's address to the Border State representatives: "Appeal to Border State Representatives to Favor Compensated Emancipation," *Collected Works of Abraham Lincoln*, vol. 5, 317–19.

pages 57–58 Majority reply from Border State: "Border State Congressmen to Abraham Lincoln," Monday July 14, 1862, posted at The Abraham Lincoln Papers at the Library of Congress, memory.loc.gov/ammem/alhtml/malhome.html.

page 58 Militia Act: Freedmen & Southern Society Project, http://www.history.umd.edu/Freedmen/milact.htm.

pages 58–59 second Confiscation Act: *From Property to Person*, 257–61.

page 60 Lincoln's address to black delegation: "Address on Colonization to a Deputation of Negroes," *Collected Works of Abraham Lincoln*, vol. 5, 370–75.

page 61 "great truth," "the mild servitude . . . ," "squelch them," and "caused the war": "What Is to be Done with the Negroes, and What with the Abolitionists?" *New York Herald*, August 29, 1862, 4.

page 62 "A spectacle, as . . .": "The President on African Colonization," *The Liberator*, August 22, 1862, 134.

page 62 "No, Mr. President . . .": "The President and His Speeches," *Douglass' Monthly*, September 1862, 707.

page 62 "Let the President . . .": "Mrs. Frances E. Watkins Harper on the War and the President's Colonization Scheme," *The Christian Recorder*, September 27, 1862, 153.

page 63 Greeley's letter to Lincoln: "Horace Greeley to Abraham Lincoln, August 1[9], 1862 (Clipping of Letter; endorsed by Lincoln)" posted at The Abraham Lincoln Papers at the Library of Congress, memory.loc.gov/ammem/alhtml/malhome.html.

pages 63–64 Lincoln's letter to Greeley: "To Horace Greeley," *Collected Works of Abraham Lincoln*, vol. 5, 388–89.

pages 64–65 *Tribune* report on cabinet meeting: "From Washington," *New-York Daily Tribune*, August 22, 1862, 5.

page 67 "extreme exercise of . . .": *Team of Rivals*, 466.

page 68 description of Carpenter painting: *United States Senate Catalogue of Fine Art*, 116–21.

page 69 "the effort to . . . loss of slaves": draft of the Preliminary Emancipation Proclamation. New York State Library, http://www.nysl.nysed.gov/library/features/ep/transcript.htm.

page 70 "OUR ARMS VICTORIOUS": *Boston Evening Transcript*, September 19, 1862, 1.

page 70 "GREAT VICTORY": *New York Times*, September 20, 1862, 1.

page 70 "I think the time . . . Maker": Salmon P. Chase. Holograph journal, open to September 22, 1862. Salmon Chase Papers, Manuscript Division, Library of Congress (154) Digital ID #al0154.

page 71 "GOD BLESS ABRAHAM LINCOLN!": *The Civil War: Primary Documents*, 128.

page 72 description of Volck etching: Vorenberg, *The Emancipation Proclamation*, 66–67.

page 73 description of Blythe painting: Miscellaneous materials provided by Carnegie Museum of Art.

Part III: "The Trump of Jubilee"

page 74 on *Watch Meeting*: *Art in the White House*, 158.

page 75 "We were waiting . . .": *Life and Times of Frederick Douglass* in *Frederick Douglass: Autobiographies*, 791.

page 77 Lincoln's December 1862 Message to Congress: "Annual Message to Congress," *Collected Works of Abraham Lincoln*, vol. 5, 518–37.

page 78 on Judge Russell at *Boston Journal*: "The Emancipation Proclamation," *New York Times*, October 16, 1884, 2.

page 78 on Tremont Temple celebration: *Frederick Douglass*, 215.

page 78 on celebration at Music Hall: "Proclamation-Day in Boston," *The Liberator*, January 9, 1863, 7.

page 78 Emerson's "Boston Hymn": *The Liberator*, January 30, 1863, 19.

pages 78–79 on the Stearns' John Brown party: "How Boston Received the Emancipation Proclamation," *The American Review of Reviews*, February 1913, 177–78.

page 79 on Turner and the Emancipation Proclamation: *The Negro's Civil War*, 50.

pages 80–83 Annotations on the Proclamation: *The Fiery Trial*, 241–44 and *Lincoln's Emancipation Proclamation*, 178–81.

pages 84–85 on celebration at Port Royal: *Army Life in a Black Regiment*, 40–41.

page 85 on Harriet Tubman probably at the Port Royal celebration: *Harriet Tubman*, 54.

page 86 "The most glorious . . .": *The Journals of Charlotte Forten Grimké*, 428–29.

page 87 "paraded through the principal streets": "News from Fortress Monroe," *New York Times*, January 4, 1863, 5.

page 87 on Cornish and the parade in Key West, Florida: "Interesting from Key West," *New York Herald*, February 11, 1863, 8.

page 88 "It was not logic . . .": *Life and Times of Frederick Douglass* in *Frederick Douglass: Autobiographies*, 791.

page 88 Harper's poem: *A Brighter Coming Day*, 186.

Epilogue

page 90 "Slavery has existed . . .": "Remarks of Frederick Douglass at Zion Church on Sunday 28, of Dec.," *Douglass' Monthly*, January 1863, 770.

page 91 "all the moral . . .": Guelzo, *Lincoln's Emancipation Proclamation*, 2.

page 97 "the very intelligent . . . cause as soldiers": "Last Public Address," *Collected Works of Abraham Lincoln*, vol. 8, 403.

page 97 "That is the last . . .": Donald, *Lincoln*, 588.

Timeline

January 10, 1862 "The President shall acquire . . .": "News from Washington," *New York Times*, January 10, 1862, 1.

January 12, 1863 "forever impossible": "The Rebel Message," *New York Herald*, January 17, 1863, 1.

October 17, 1863 "information has reached . . .": "The Experimental Black Colony," *New York Times*, October 17, 1863, http://www.nytimes.com/1863/10/17/news/washington-our-special-washington-dispatches-eastern-shore-counties-virginia.html?scp=1&sq=colonists&st=p.

November 19, 1863 Battle of Gettysburg data: "Gettysburg," CWSAC Battle Summaries, http://www.nps.gov/history/hps/abpp/battles/pa002.htm. Gettysburg Address: "Bliss Copy," at http://www.papersofabrahamlincoln.org/Gettysburg%20Address.htm.

December 22, 1864 Sherman's telegram: "William T. Sherman to Abraham Lincoln, Thursday, December 22, 1864," The Abraham Lincoln Papers at the Library of Congress (online).

February 7, 1865 "spirited and admirable painting": "Abraham Lincoln to William Lloyd Garrison, [February 7, 1865], The Abraham Lincoln Papers at the Library of Congress (online).

March 4, 1865 "With malice toward none . . .": "Second Inaugural Address," *Collected Works of Abraham Lincoln*, vol. 8, 333.

SELECTED SOURCES

Basler, Roy P., ed. *The Collected Works of Abraham Lincoln.* http://quod.lib.umich.edu/l/lincoln/.

Bennett, Lerone, Jr. *Forced into Glory: Abraham Lincoln's White Dream.* Chicago: Johnson Publishing, 2000.

Blair, William A., and Karen Fisher Younger, eds. *Lincoln's Proclamation: Emancipation Reconsidered.* Chapel Hill: University of North Carolina Press, 2009.

Blassingame, John W. *Slave Testimony: Two Centuries of Letters, Speeches, Interviews, and Autobiographies.* Baton Rouge: Louisiana State University Press, 1996.

Chapman, Maria Weston, ed. *Songs of the Free, and Hymns of Christian Freedom.* Boston: Isaac Knapp, 1836.

Collins, Lewis and Richard H. *History of Kentucky* vol. 1, Covington, KY: Collins & Co, 1878.

Cox, LaWanda. *Lincoln and Black Freedom: A Study in Presidential Leadership.* Columbia: University of South Carolina Press, 1993.

Donald, David Herbert. *Lincoln.* New York: Simon & Schuster, 1995.

Foner, Eric. *The Fiery Trial: Abraham Lincoln and American Slavery.* New York: W.W. Norton, 2010.

———. *Forever Free: The Story of Emancipation and Reconstruction.* New York: Vintage, 2006.

———, ed. *Our Lincoln: New Perspectives on Lincoln and His World.* New York: W.W. Norton, 2009.

Foster, Frances Smith. *A Brighter Coming Day: A Frances Ellen Watkins Harper Reader.* New York: The Feminist Press, 1990.

Franklin, John Hope. *The Emancipation Proclamation.* Wheeling, IL: Harlan Davidson, 1995.

Gates, Henry Louis, Jr., volume editor. *Frederick Douglass: Autobiographies.* New York: Library of America, 1994.

Gienapp, William E., ed. *The Civil War and Reconstruction: A Documentary Collection.* New York: W.W. Norton, 2001.

Goodwin, Doris Kearns. *Team of Rivals: The Political Genius of Abraham Lincoln.* New York: Simon & Schuster, 2006.

Gougeon, Len and Joel Myerson, eds. *Emerson's Antislavery Writings.* New Haven: Yale University Press, 1995.

Guelzo, Allen C. *Lincoln's Emancipation Proclamation: The End of Slavery in America.* New York: Simon & Schuster, 2006.

Hanlon, Christopher. "Embodied Eloquence, the Sumner Assault, and the Transatlantic Cable," *American Literature*, vol 82, no. 3, September 2010. 489–518.

Higginson, Thomas Wentworth. *Army Life in a Black Regiment.* Boston: Field, Osgood & Co., 1870.

Holzer, Harold, Edna Greene Medford, and Frank J. Williams. *The Emancipation Proclamation: Three Views.* Baton Rouge: Louisiana State University Press, 2006.

Humez, Jean M. *Harriet Tubman: The Life and the Life Stories.* Madison: University of Wisconsin Press, 2003.

Kachun, Mitch. *Festivals of Freedom: Memory and Meaning in African American Emancipation Celebrations, 1808–1915.* Amherst: University of Massachusetts Press, 2003.

Kloss, William et al. *Art in the White House: A Nation's Pride.* New York: Abrams, 1994.

Kloss, William and Diane K. Skvarla. U.S. Senate Commission on Art. *United States Senate Catalogue of Fine Art.* D.C.: Government Printing Office, 2002.

Lester, C. Edwards. *Life and Public Services of Charles Sumner.* New York: United States Publishing Co., 1874.

McFeely, William S. *Frederick Douglass.* New York: W.W. Norton, 1995.

McPherson, James M. *Battle Cry of Freedom: The Civil War Era.* New York: Oxford University Press, 2003.

———. *The Negro's Civil War.* New York: Ballantine, 1991.

Phillips, Wendell. *Speech, Lectures, and Letters.* Boston: Lee and Shepard, 1872.

Pierce, Edward L., ed. *Memoir and Letters of Charles Sumner,* vol. 4. 2nd ed. Boston: Roberts Brothers, 1894.

Quarles, Benjamin. *Lincoln and The Negro*. New York: Da Capo Press, 1991.

Reid, Whitelaw. *After the War: A Southern Tour, May 1, 1865 to May 1, 1866*. London: Sampson Low, Son & Marston, 1866.

Risley, Ford. *The Civil War: Primary Documents on Events from 1860 to 1865*. Westport, CT: Greenwood Press, 2004.

Schmidt, Lewis G. "From Slavery to Freedom and Success: Sandy Cornish and Lillah Cornish," *Florida Keys Sea Heritage Journal*, Spring 1994, 1, 12–15.

Siddali, Silvana R. *From Property to Person: Slavery and the Confiscation Acts, 1861–1862*. Baton Rouge: Louisiana State University Press, 2005.

Stevenson, Brenda, ed. *The Journals of Charlotte Forten Grimké*. New York: Oxford University Press, 1989.

Striner, Richard. *Father Abraham: Lincoln's Relentless Struggle to End Slavery*. New York: Oxford University Press, 2007.

Villard, Fanny Garrison. "How Boston Received the Emancipation Proclamation," *The American Review of Reviews*, February 1913.

Vorenberg, Michael. *The Emancipation Proclamation: A Brief History with Documents*. Boston: Bedford/St. Martin's, 2010.

———. *Final Freedom: The Civil War, the Abolition of Slavery, and the Thirteenth Amendment*. Cambridge: Cambridge University Press, 2004.

ACKNOWLEDGMENTS

I am so grateful to my editor, Howard Reeves, for his commitment and for being, once again, so wonderful to work with.

I am also deeply indebted to other members of the Abrams Books for Young Readers family, people who routinely go above and beyond: editorial assistant Jenna Pocius; managing editor Jim Armstrong; associate managing editor Jen Graham; designer Maria Middleton; production manager Alison Gervais; senior publicist Mary Ann Zissimos; marketing and publicity coordinator Laura Mihalick; and marketing and publicity director Jason Wells. I thank you all so much for your attention to detail and for your brilliance. I'd be remiss if I didn't also thank copyeditor Anne Heausler, proofreader Rob Sternitzky, and fact-checker David Webster.

This book also had the benefit of the enlightening minds of law professor Bobby Thomas, who helped me unpack legalese, and Dr. Stephen Kenney, director of Boston's Commonwealth Museum, who also read the manuscript and gave me such thoughtful, meaningful comments.

IMAGE CREDITS

INDEX

Page references in italics refer to figures, illustrations, or photographs.

be prosecuted. And, as a fit and necessary military measure for effecting this purpose, I, as Commander-in-Chief of the Army and Navy of the United States, do order and declare that on the first day of January, in the year of our Lord one thousand eight hundred and sixty three, all persons held as slaves in any State or States, wherein the constitutional authority of the United States shall not then be practically recognized, submitted to, and maintained, shall then, thenceforward, and forever, be free;

be prosecuted. And, as a fit and necessary war measure for suppressing said rebellion, do, on this first day of January, in the year of our Lord one thousand eight hundred and sixty three, and in accordance with my purpose so to do publicly proclaimed for the full period of one hundred days, from the day first above mentioned, order and designate as the States and parts of States wherein the people thereof respectively, are this day in rebellion against the United States, the following, to wit: